Manufacturing, Product, Solutions:

Adapt your business to a changing world

Netanel Raisch

Manufacturing, Product, Solutions: Adapt your business to a changing world/ by Netanel Raisch

Edition 1.0

Cover images: iStockphoto

Copyright © 2013 by Netanel Raisch

All rights reserved.

www.netanelraisch.com

Raisch, Netanel.

MANUFACTURING, PRODUCT, SOLUTIONS

I am only in the beginning of the journey

But I already want to thank to all the people

Who helped me to reach this point,

And especially my family

Contents

Contents	4
Preface - The objective of the book	6
Introduction	12
Chapter Minus One	14
The companies	25
Pricing	32
Knowledge	48
Location	53
The theory global effect	66
Operations Management	73
Documentation	79
The Company Employees	84
Sales	93
R&D	97
Marketing	110
The Client	129
Advertising	138

MANUFACTURING, PRODUCT, SOLUTIONS

The Brand	147
Intellectual Property	156
The Company Structure	167
Quality Control	173
Service	184
Warranty	193
International Marketing	198
Presence on the Internet	208
The Sales Team	214
Marketing Icons	218
The Planning Horizon	222
Regulation	230
In Lieu of a Summary	235
Epilogue	239

Preface - The objective of the book

People who seek a simple and quick way to get rich, or who seek an innovative method to make a profit, will not find tips in this book. My objective in writing the book is to provide a different perspective about the types of companies on the market, in the era of information and globalization, in order to give each manager the chance to examine the company he or she runs, and to get ideas about components and aspects that may be altered so as to make the company more profitable.

The book presents a theory, according to which any company may be identified as focusing on one of the following categories: manufacturing, product or solutions. In contrast to Mendeleev's periodic table, which tried to bring a certain order to all of the materials in the world, including those unknown materials that had yet to be discovered, my table is complete and has no room for additional categories (perhaps because as a manager, I tend to be wary of tables with more than three categories). Nevertheless, like Mendeleev, I too strive to establish some order – in the business world. The objective of this proposed order is to demonstrate that differences that distinguish between companies in the various categories exist in all of the components of the company. This observation is not self-evident today.

What the three company types in my model have in common is their goal and their method: The goal is to create the maximum possible value for the shareholders, and the method is to sell whatever the client is prepared to pay for. All other company components differ according to the company's focus, be it manufacturing, product or solutions.

There is nothing in this book that you could not have gathered from your own observations of the business world and related publications. Nonetheless (and at the risk of sounding exaggeratedly grandiose), millions of apples fell before Newton asked himself "why?". Finding the rule does not change the way in which apples fall from trees, but it enables us to plan new things based on this theory. I hope my theory introduces some order into our understanding of companies and the way they work, while demonstrating that viewing a company from a new perspective and through a new definition affects how we perceive all of its components.

I shall try to relate in my book to all of the types of companies that currently exist in the global business world. Indeed, in today's world, a company may be established in the US, have shareholders all over the world and a development center based in Israel. It may manufacture its products in China, send them to distribution centers on five different continents, while providing support to clientele in India and maintaining branches of local support in other parts of the world. Alternatively, businesses may exist solely as virtual entities on the Internet, where clients and sellers meet directly, without any need for brand recognition or company representatives.

The global perspective of this book and its method of classification enable each company to identify itself within the theory, and derive benefit from understanding its position in the order of categories. Practically, managers can obtain advice on the actions they should take and the aspects or components of the company that should be altered in order to improve the company's positioning in the business world.

Different kinds of companies may exist anywhere in the world; nevertheless, as will be explained in detail in a different section of this book, there are reasons why certain countries are more attractive than others to manufacturers. The book will also clarify why the fact that these countries rely on such companies and consequently have a production-based economy effectively limits their ability to develop and increase profits on a national level. Thus, for example, China, the global manufacturing superpower, as well as Brazil and India, relies heavily on large companies that control a major part of the world's manufacturing needs, but consequently it can enjoy only narrow profit margins. The Chinese government has come to understand the difficulties that stem from its role as the world's greatest manufacturer, and is encouraging Chinese companies to purchase technologies and businesses outside of China.

The Chinese government, of course, came to a very wise conclusion; however, I believe that what this book has to offer goes beyond the insight provided by China. The aim of this book, then, is to address the intuitive understanding that stepping away from the role of manufacturer requires more than the acquisition of new equipment and advanced technologies. It requires a new way of thinking. To this end, I propose the paradigm of "manufacturing– product – solutions". To make the transition to a solutions-based company requires more than merely acquiring Western brands or natural resources: it requires changing thought patterns, making the shift to a different paradigm. I am convinced that any Chinese company that opts to apply the new paradigm to both the company's leadership and structure will succeed in becoming a solutions-based company and, moreover, will have the world's consumers pounding at its doors.

Likewise, this book can serve as an important auxiliary tool for companies in the Western Hemisphere, enabling them to understand their advantages in view of the competition from the East, which threatens to invade and conquer their market. It also provides practical ideas and suggestions for activities that can help companies expand and thrive, not only in terms of their virtual presence, but also in their day-to-day, on-the-ground functioning, so as to produce value and create employment opportunities in their own countries. It is clear that having an educated population that possesses both extensive knowledge and high intellectual abilities is an obvious advantage; unfortunately, the abilities of such populations are not necessarily used in ways that bring the optimal benefit to their countries. This book shows how, by adopting a slightly different perspective, company managers and employees can work together to generate a lot more value for the client. When your clients are willing to pay more for a perceived value, two positive outcomes are virtually guaranteed: higher profits for shareholders, and a profit margin that allows you to hire local employees, instead of seeking cheaper laborers in other countries.

My objective in writing this book was to allow people to look at the business world through my eyes. I have helped friends, suppliers and clients understand and operate according to the manufacturing-product-solutions paradigm, and I would be delighted to know that you have benefited from it as well.

Introduction

The history of the evolution of this book begins with my decision to leave my job at a company which I worked (we'll call that company *Feb*). I took a vacation, during which I intended to plan my next step, and figure out where I would want to work. Two weeks before this planned vacation, I ran into with the owner of one of *Feb*'s suppliers (we'll call that company *Ner*), who generously offered me a job. He actually offered me any job I wanted, as long as I agreed to join either the marketing or the research and development department in his company. My gut instinct was to decline. Basically, the company consisted of a large sewing workshop, which manufactured high quality products at competitive prices. In other words, there would be no real need for either a highly skilled marketing professional who could initiate new and significant processes or for an R&D manager who would venture to suggest products requiring long-term development. I replied that I would reach a decision by the time I returned from my vacation.

During this leave, I tried to analyze the reason behind my instinct to turn down such a generous offer. I tried to organize my thoughts, by asking myself concrete questions. "If I took a job as vice-president of marketing in Ner, what course of action would I want to take?" "What could I contribute in a company that is virtually unknown, its name unrecognized, a company whose label communicates no more than the simple message of 'price per quality'?" " If I became vice-president of research and development, what could I develop in a company whose knowledge and scope were in sewing?" "Why shouldn't I want to work at a company that was prepared to offer me any job I wanted?"

This book is the product of that analysis, a description of what I knew intuitively, the reasons behind the gut reaction that prevented me from saying "yes" to the owner of Ner. I hope to successfully convey my thoughts to you.

Chapter Minus One

Let me try to describe Ner for you. Ner is located in an industrial zone, and consists mainly of a large sewing workshop of enormous capacity. The job orders Ner receives include measurements and material specifications, in return for which Ner charges the customer a price that is based on the cost of raw materials, with some percentage added for overhead and labor. The company is not interested in the product, its purpose or its use.

Ner is an amazing family business, with wonderful owners and a high sales turnover rate. But in the end, its only advantage in the market in which it competes is the price it charges for the manufactured product. When I met with the owners, I posed this question: "If a competitor offers your client a price that is 5% lower than yours, would the client remain loyal or move to the competition?" Without hesitation, the answer was: "The client would accept the competing offer, even though we may offer better service".

When I asked: "How much have you invested in R&D this year?" they said: "A lot, we produced samples of new products for our clients, with no remuneration". After a short discussion, the owners agreed with me that producing samples for clients should go under marketing costs and not R&D costs, since this expenditure does not produce unique knowledge for the company, which gives them an edge in the market where they operate.

Based on this discussion and the answers I'd heard, I began to formulate an understanding of what made Ner different from other companies I was familiar with, and I started to develop a sense of how I could distinguish between companies, in general.

My first and basic understanding was that Ner does not have a product. It cannot put its logo on any one product, since it manufactures products that the client then sells to the end customers under its own brand name. In many cases, Ner even sews the client's label onto the products it manufactures.

The only thing Ner sells, therefore, is the ability to manufacture a certain kind of product. It sells the work hours of its employees and the service of importing and storing the raw materials. It does not have the knowledge required to either make a new product or to improve any of the products it already makes.

This led to my first definition. Ner is a manufacturing company. It sells production, and the most basic way to distinguish a manufacturing company from other types of companies is by asking: "Does the company produce according to the client's specifications?" It doesn't matter if the client is a conglomerate or a private customer; in the case of a manufacturing company, the answer is always affirmative. Ner is a manufacturing company. It produces products according to the instructions of the client, per its regulations, and it produces nothing without getting the client's signature on the designs. Both a tailor on the street corner who shortens people's trousers and Foxacon, which employs half a million people, are production companies, since they perform according to the client's specifications and make no decisions about the object they produce.

By contrast, a company that manufactures finished products based on its own knowledge can be called a product-based company. This type of company is the type most familiar to the general public, although it does not necessarily sell its products directly to the consumer. We are exposed to product-based companies in many realms of our lives: We see their names on the supermarket shelves and in newspaper advertisements. In some cases a product-based company's brand name might appear on a particular product, even though the company is associated only with a certain component that is integrated into the final product.

A product-based company knows how to produce and sell what it manufactures. It invests a lot of money in research and development, in order to make a better and more advanced product. Its ultimate goal is to be significantly more profitable than its competitors, who sell an equivalent product. To attain this goal, the company's leverage must be the price that the customer is willing to pay for the advantage of using *this company's* product, as opposed to that of competing companies. The profit does not come from varying production costs, since in a perfect market; two companies that produce similar products which offer essentially the same benefits will incur similar costs. For example, the cost of car manufacturing in Japan will be similar for all Japanese car companies. In an open market with free competition, this leads to low profit margins. In this situation, one company may attempt to sell greater quantities by lowering prices by only a small percentage, which in turn typically leads to price wars among all players in the given market, following which the price usually settles at a relatively low level.

Companies understand that they cannot increase their net profit solely by selling more products; therefore, they attempt to distinguish themselves by what is known as intangible assets. Such assets may be attained, for example, by creating a prestigious brand or developing company-owned patents. Actions such as these serve to emphasize the product's intangible factor, which in turn increases the product's value in the eyes of the consumer, who therefore is willing to pay a higher price. The intangible factor may be expressed in various aspects of the product, such as simpler operation, added functionalities, or a feature that addresses a specific need of the customer. The customer may be totally unaware of the actions the company took and the costs it incurred to provide the solution or the intangible asset.

The intangible asset is clear, for example, when we buy a watch. A $10 watch and a $10,000 watch fulfill the same function: they tell time. Nevertheless, we may be willing to pay a lot more for a prestigious watch that costs $10,000, because of an intangible benefit, such as a declaration of social status, which is associated with the brand name. Thus, we have defined the company that sells the prestigious watch as a *product-based company*. How might we define a company that sells a product with innovative functionalities that cannot be found in similar products competing in the same market?

It is self-evident that if two companies sell similar products, yet one of them sells the product as is, while the other sells innovative versions of the same item, the business operations of the two do not pertain to the same category. A company that makes use of unique knowledge, inaccessible to other companies (protected by patent or copyrights) operates at a more sophisticated level, and therefore we may consider it a *unique product company*.

An example of a unique product company is Apple, which developed the iPhone and introduced a whole new world of experiences into customers' use of cellular phones. Apple cannot be defined as just another product-based company in the cellular market, competing with others by offering lower prices. It is a unique company, which typically needs to educate the consumer about its superior product and explain the additional benefits that can be derived from this product, as compared to the market alternatives.

A unique product company provides a product that other companies cannot copy for various reasons, and is therefore more sophisticated than regular product-based companies. However, there are also companies that not only offer a high quality product but also claim responsibility for the quality of the result attained by using the product. Such companies operate at a level of sophistication above that of product-based and unique product companies. We define these as *solutions-based companies*.

Solutions-based companies learn the problems of the clients and accumulate relevant knowledge, which they then translate into new developments, not only of products but also of features and functionalities that allow for optimal and innovative use of existing products. These companies mainly sell their knowledge and, therefore, their profit margins are especially high. In many cases, the solution sold by the company consists of a product (which the company may purchase from a product-based company) and the promise of providing the customer with ongoing, high quality services affiliated with the product throughout the predefined purchase period. The purpose of providing an ongoing service is to ensure that the use of the solution in fact provides the client with the desired outcome.

To examine the proposition regarding the category of solutions-based companies, let us take Teva as a case study. Teva is a global pharmaceutical company that currently markets about 1250 different drugs, of these, 1248 are generic. This means that Teva produces a precise duplicate of drugs developed by other companies as soon as the patents for the original drugs have expired. Teva has developed only two drugs for which it owns the patents. In 2009, Teva's sales came to $13.9 billion; 70% of that sum came from the sale of the 1248 generic drugs, while 30% came from selling one single drug – Copaxone. Findings from the profit analysis were even more amazing than those derived from the sales analysis: 50% of Teva's profits that year were from the sale of a single patented drug and the remaining 50% came from the sale of the 1248 generic drugs. This means that a single patent-protected drug can be worth 1248 times the value of an unprotected one.

The example of Teva demonstrates the significance of a company's intellectual assets. These assets are what transform a product-based company into a unique product company, placing it in a higher category. Yet, is Teva merely a product-based company or a unique product company? Well, it may come as a surprise, but Teva in fact does provide an affiliated service, to make sure that patients that use Copaxone administer the product appropriately. Although Teva cannot guarantee 100% success; nevertheless, I believe it should be considered both a product-based and a solutions-based company.

Let us first see if Teva's competitors can produce the same product as it does. As we saw, Teva imitates 1248 drugs of other companies, which indicates that these drugs could be manufactured also by competitors. That is why the profit percentage for these drugs is small. In addition, Teva has also two patent-protected drugs, which its competitors are unable to produce. This allows for a wide profit margin from the sale of these drugs. The patent protected products are what make Teva a unique product company, in contrast to a solutions-based company. Although Teva does not provide a guarantee that the patient's condition will improve after using the drug, it habitually provides patient support during the period of use through independent tertiary agents, namely, the treating physicians. Furthermore, in an effort to ensure the desired outcome from the use of its unique product, it also provides its own services to guide new, first-time customers in the proper administration and use of this product.

Before Teva received approval for marketing the patented drug, it had to undergo a series of trials, supervised by statutory agencies such as the FDA, to ensure that the drug delivers the expected results, while ensuring the user's safety. Based on the outcome of the clinical trials, Teva, aided by the FDA approval, can now guarantee, (to a limited extent) the drug's effectiveness, assuming proper use. Even if a company does not provide its own affiliated services to aid the first time user, as Teva does, the patient is accompanied throughout the period of use of the product by a third party, namely the attending physician, who is involved in ensuring that the product is used properly, thus providing this service on behalf of Teva. The specialist treating these patients receives from Teva the required knowledge to ensure the patient's optimal benefit from using the drug. Naturally, the doctor also follows up on the patient's progress, and based on clinical outcome may change the dosages or methods of use, so that the client derives the maximum benefit from the drug.

The conclusion, therefore, is that Teva's style of operations matches the category of a solutions-based company, in addition to its being a product-based company. The distinction introduced here between manufacturing companies, product-based companies, and solutions-based companies may also be apparent between the existing divisions within a single company. This type of divergence within a company usually signals a healthy development, marking the company's shift from a limited focus to a more ambitious scope, either by adding a product-oriented approach to its existing manufacturing capacities, or by providing solutions and services to accompany its existing product.

To summarize, if we analyze the companies on the market, we can distinguish three types of companies, where the first criterion for distinction is the product sold.

- Manufacturing Company – a company that derives the major portion of its income from tasks performed according to the client's specifications.

- Product-based Company – a company that derives the major portion of its income from selling the finished products it developed.

- Solutions-based Company – a company that derives the major portion of its income from selling solutions, which include the product and specific knowledge (of either the clients' behavior or of aspects related to manufacturing or development), while taking responsibility for the result obtained after purchase.

A unique product company does not merit a separate category, since in some cases it behaves like a product-based company, while in others it resembles a solutions-based company. I am sure the readers will be able to distinguish in each case whether the unique product company functions more like a product-based company or like a solutions-based company.

The companies

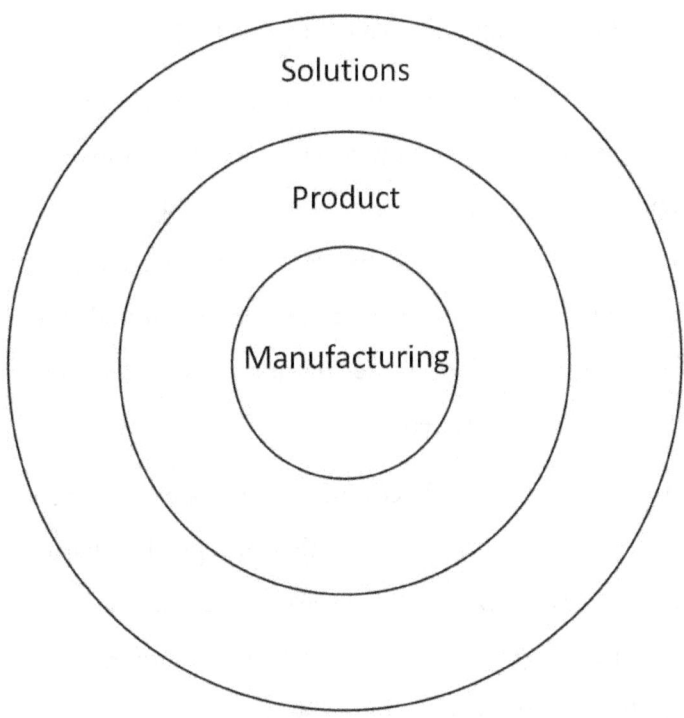

In the diagram, each of the concentric circles represents a business type category. The concentric structure indicates that a solutions-based company may incorporate within its operations the activities of a product-based company, which in turn may subsume a manufacturing company. There may be some exceptions, but this is generally the rule.

To clarify, let's consider the example of a company that provides cellular communication. This company sells solutions – the ability to communicate using cellular phones or similar devices. What is the actual product that this company sells? It sells air time. What does the company manufacture? It produces radio waves at a cellular frequency, through which the data are passed.

When we speak on a cellular phone and use the company's solution services, we don't stop to consider the company's manufacturing operations or its product. We focus on our ability to use the device in our hands to communicate with another equivalent device located anywhere around the globe. Without the services of the solutions-based company, our device would be worthless.

Thus, the solutions-based company addresses a given problem in a manner different from that of a product-based company. The latter provides one aspect of the solution, namely, a specific product that the client must operate in order to obtain a complete solution, whereas, the solutions-based company provides a long-term commitment to provide clients with an overall solution for a predefined period. The solutions-based company possesses knowledge and provides a framework that offers customers a solution that extends beyond anything that the purchase of a product could address.

Another distinguishing feature of a solutions-based company is that it does not actually have to produce or develop anything tangible; it is possible that the best solution to a client's specific problem can be addressed merely by purchasing products from other companies and then assembling and selling them as a complete integrated system. In this case, the solutions-based company sells nothing but knowledge. An example of this type of solutions-based company is that of insurance companies. Insurance companies sell insurance to clients they have never met, by means of a product-based company, namely the insurance agency, and they underwrite other large companies, which in turn provide customers with the coverage promised them by the solutions-based insurance companies.

Returning now to our previous example, it appears that the service provided by cellular communication companies is one of the most complex products for customers to grasp. The product, which may or may not include a cellular device, is priced at various rates per minute of use, with rates varying based on type of use and type of client. Thus, there is one rate for making and receiving calls, another for sending text messages, yet another for surfing the Internet, receiving electronic mail, downloading games, and insuring the device. For each of the mentioned operations, there are at least two rate categories, a business rate and a private rate. Often the complexity of this pricing system makes it difficult to compare one company's rates with those of the competition. As clients, we have no idea what is the actual cost of the product we receive and, more often than not, we do not even bother to understand what it is we are paying for. Nevertheless, most of us are willing to pay, just to have at our fingertips the solution we need --when we need it.

Obviously, cellular communication companies are not the only companies to exert this spellbinding power over us. Our banks, credit card companies, insurance companies, health insurance providers, hospitals can cause us to agree to pay and overlook the cost. Basically, any company whose solutions we the clients deem necessary exerts the same power over its clients.

A major and essential difference between solutions- and product-based companies is the company's liability for the result of the purchase. This differentiating factor affects the quality of the ongoing relationship between company and customers. Typically, the client encounters the product-based company at the point of sale, whereby the forging of a potential relationship between client and company requires that the client compare among alternative options, in order to understand each product's advantages, as well as its pricing schedule. The eventual solution that the product provides is derived through the client's use of the product.

Companies that sell devices that include several components, perhaps a combination of tangible and intangible properties, also belong to the category of product-based companies. Thus, for example, a company that sells computers, which require software and services for their operation, is a product-based company. Almost anything that can be directly purchased by the end customer is bought from a product-based company. Regardless of whether the product-based company handles its product manufacturing in-house or by outsourcing, by definition, a product-based company always retains some component of the manufacturing process, even if it is only the R&D aspect.

What about your car? If you ask, you will be told that it was made by Toyota, Mazda, Ford or Renault, but where was each of its parts manufactured? In fact, only few parts are manufactured by the car companies, and even the assembly is often conducted at a location other than the company plant. Typically, each of the vehicle's parts is produced by a different company, which specializes in manufacturing that particular part. The only thing these parts have in common is the product-based company that sells you the car, and places its emblem on the hood of the car. The consumer is unaware of the companies that produced the various parts of car and will probably never know their names. Only if a problem arises that is brought to public attention will the names of the manufacturing companies be mentioned. Thus, for example, following the "gas pedal crisis"[1], Toyota, apologized for the failure and announced that the faulty part had been produced by CTS Corporation, while Toyota itself took responsibility for failing to adequately supervise the quality of the work done by the manufacturer. Until this affair was made public, Toyota's clients knew nothing about the CTS Corporation or its relationship with Toyota's products. It is precisely this aspect, that is, the absence of any relationship between the company and the consumer, which places the company in the category of manufacturer. Thus, manufacturing companies take advantage of their size and location to sell products at the lowest possible price, so as to attract product- and solutions-based companies.

Manufacturing companies do not sell products, and certainly not solutions; therefore, in terms of their gains and brand strength, they are at the bottom of the pyramid. If it weren't for the media publicizing the unfortunate incidents, I doubt any of Toyota's clients would have cared one way or

---

[1] Retrieved from http://www.motortrend.com/features/auto_news/2010/112_1001_toyota_recall_crisis/viewall.html on April 6, 2013.

another which gas pedal supplier Toyota used. Here again, the fact that the manufacturer ultimately is not accountable to the end consumer gives Toyota its strength vis-à-vis the manufacturing companies: Due to its purchasing power, Toyota can demand a low price from manufacturers while affording itself a wider profit margin.

Pricing

Manufacturing Companies

Feb decided to initiate an organizational change. It wanted to change from a company producing "simple" products, to the production of "smarter" ones. In this process, the company wanted to increase the profitability of its unique products and to provide the client with solutions that would be far better than those offered by the competition. One of the difficulties encountered during the process was the need to incorporate a new way of presenting the price to the client. Until the change took place, clients were quoted a per-square-meter price, which had the unfortunate effect of diminishing the product's image and enabling potential customers to compare *Feb* per-unit prices with those of the competition. However, with the transition to more sophisticated products, the per-unit comparison would not properly project the potential benefit customers could expect from these products, and therefore such a comparison would only lead to a limited representation of the products. The change required the company to cease giving per-unit quotes and to embark on a process for raising the prices on all of its products. In hindsight, this was the correct decision, but at the time it was very difficult to implement.

The reason that changes in pricing are extremely difficult to implement is that the price shift projects outwardly: It is equivalent to a public announcement about the change taking place inside the company. The price quoted to the client embodies what the company thinks of itself and of its position within the market in which it operates. In addition, the increased price also reflects the accrued cost of planning and implementing the change, including recruitment of new R&D employees, and hiring marketing personnel who have experience selling more sophisticated products. The pricing and its presentation to the client enables the company to observe, evaluate and decide where it is currently – in relation to the goals of the process, and how it wants to proceed from this stage.

Let me describe the stage of price presentation that is characteristic of a manufacturing company such as *Ner* in dialogue form.

Client: How much would 50 units of 2x2 m. sewn canvases cost?

Salesperson: The price is NIS 100 per unit.

Client: Are you kidding? How on earth did you come up with such a price?

Salesperson: The raw materials cost NIS 20 per square meter-- Right? This is for the material you buy from us in rolls. In addition, there is cutting, sewing and packaging of 50 units, about 20 minutes of work per unit, right? A work hour, with all related expenses costs around NIS 60, so now do you see how I end up with 100 NIS per unit?

Client: OK, but it's still expensive.

Salesperson: Well, let my check with my supervisor and see what I can do.

After a quick check with the manager, the salesperson gets back to the client:

"Listen, only for you, and as we are talking about a large order of 50 units, I can offer you a reduced price of NIS 95 per unit, as a one-time offer. Are you in?

Client: Yes, you have a deal.

Let us analyze the dialogue and examine the pricing process.

The question apparently is, doesn't *Ner* want to make a profit? Every company aims to create value for its stockholders, usually monetary value. *Ner* should make a profit, but according to the calculations presented by the salesperson, it makes no profit, and after the discount negotiated with the manager, the company supposedly loses money on the order.

As I can assure you, *Ner* is a solid and profitable company; therefore, let us examine the untold story behind product pricing in a manufacturing company, and thus understand the difference between production cost and price, and how these companies manage to make a profit.

The data provided to the client are clear and enable the salesperson to quote a price on the spot. They are discussing 50 units of four square meters each, made of a certain material, the price of which is known, requiring stitching around the edges, a total of 8 meters per unit, the cost of which is also easily calculated.

This client was not prepared to accept the unit price offered; yet, rather than walk away and take his business elsewhere, he wanted to get a breakdown of the costs. When clients ask for a price quote from a manufacturing company, they usually come with some idea of what price to expect, often because they have made an effort to find out what it would cost to do the job on their own. The fact that the client in the above dialogue asked for cost itemization suggests that they lack the capacity to complete the entire job alone. Indeed, no one comes to a bakery and asks to see an itemized list of the cost of making bread. Nor is this done when buying more complex and expensive products, such as an apartment or a car. Hence, clients that ask for itemized information from a manufacturing company, are considering whether they could do **part of the job** themselves.

A client that knows the cost of raw materials can consider the option of buying the material independently, supposedly for a cheaper price, and then sending it to the manufacturer to be sewn. Often a manufacturer refuses to do only part of the job, and we shall later understand why. Nevertheless, in the case of *Ner*, as well as other companies I have worked with, the job done by the manufacturer can always be split up, so that only part of the manufacturing is done in a specific company.

Once clients receive the breakdown of the costs, they are adequately equipped to check and compare prices. Thus, in the preceding dialogue, the client was first told the price of raw materials, then the time required and finally the cost of labor. With this information, a client can certainly decide whether the best option is to do the job independently, in-house, to divide up the work and do part of it alone, or to pursue other alternatives on the market. Once itemized pricing information has been handed over --free of charge, the customer is well-equipped to weigh the options and reach a decision. If following the previously presented dialogue, the client were to find another supplier whose price was NIS 105 per unit, but the itemized cost of labor was calculated differently, say at

NIS 30 per hour, the client would then be able to use this information as a leveraging factor. He would then go back to Ner and try to negotiate for a better price, based on the competitor's price per time invested, because he understands that this could save him money.

Let us now return to the earlier question: How does *Ner* make a profit? It is clear that when we pay for a product, it entails a certain percentage of profit for the manufacturer. However, manufacturers practically never include this in the cost itemization. Undoubtedly, an item listing "profit – 10%" would only invite opposition and expose the company's true costs.

Therefore, when a manufacturing company quotes the cost of raw materials and labor, these numbers already include the company's profit; in other words, the itemization is of the *cost for the client* rather than the price that manufacturer pays for raw materials and labor. The manufacturer's profit is derived from the difference between what the customer would pay if he or she did the job independently in-house and the manufacturing company's actual accrued costs, which are substantially lower than the former, due to the company's size. The size of the manufacturing company is an important factor: A very large company may need to keep an extensive stock; hence, the price at which it purchases its raw materials is apt to be significantly lower than the price the client would pay. Herein lies the first source of profit -- the manufacturer's purchasing power.

Typically, we all want to know the actual cost of the products we buy, but often the results are surprising. Let me share with you a personal experience. In a discussion with my wife about family spending cuts, she noted that buying lunch at a restaurant or even at a food stall was expensive, and that we could save some money by purchasing the ingredients at the supermarket and making sandwiches at home. After some resistance, I finally broke down and decided to examine the theory. So, one day, instead of buying a cutlet sandwich at a fast food stall, I decided to buy the ingredients at the supermarket and make my own sandwich. I bought cold cuts instead of the cutlet, a bread roll, a small box of hummus, and one tomato. As you might have guessed, the sandwich I made was more expensive than the one sold by the fast-food vendor, even without taking into account the cost of time involved in the preparation or the great variety of salads and spreads offered at the food stand. It goes without saying that a warm cutlet is tastier and hence more appetizing than cold cuts. In addition, around the canteen there are tables for customers to relax and enjoy their lunch, an option which was not available at the supermarket.

What do you think is the relevant conclusion to be drawn from this story? Did you imagine for one second that the canteen owner doesn't make a profit? Of course not! This is because food vendors function just like a manufacturing company: They enjoy an advantage of size and volume, which grants them the kind of buying power that guarantees lower rates. Thus, vendors have profited even before a single item is sold. The food vendors have other advantages, when compared to an individual engaging in a similar production process. For example, although the individual might intend to purchase minimal quantities for preparing a single sandwich, the percentage of loss or waste is greater for the individual than for the manufacturing company, in this case, the food vendor.

Back to *Ner*: as noted previously, one portion of the manufacturer's profit is derived from the difference between the cost the individual client would have to pay and the price the manufacturer was actually charged. The manufacturer's costs are lower than those of an individual client for a number of reasons:

1. The manufacturing company may be located geographically where the cost of labor is lower than it is at the client's location. As shown in previous examples, it may be located in China while the client is in the USA.

2. The manufacturer employs workers who are more skilled than the client is in performing this specific task.

3. The manufacturer is not subject to the same labor laws (if located in a different country), nor bound by agreements which would pertain to an individual client. For example, companies that hire employees on a contractual basis do not pay social and other benefits, which the individual client would be obligated to pay.

4. The manufacturer has machines and equipment, which the client is unable to access without hiring the services of another company.

As seen, the manufacturing company takes into account these differences in costs. It is also aware that it operates in a very competitive market, devoid of sentiment or loyalty. Therefore, when quoting a price, it will also take into consideration the price offered by competitors and the price range acceptable in that particular market.

Thus, a major difference between a manufacturing company and a product-based company is related to the issue of pricing. A product-based company quotes a price per service or product, and would never present the customer with a list of the itemized costs of each of the product's components. In determining the price of a product, the product-based company aims to maximize its profits, taking into account the conditions of supply and demand, rather than the actual cost of producing or purchasing it's the product's components.

Product-Based Companies

There are thousands of examples for the system of pricing products, and many books have been written on the subject, aiming to teach companies how to maximize their profits. I would like to draw your attention to the case of a company that offers a more advanced product on the market.

The answer to the question why a company would put a new product on the market while the current product is still selling well is two-fold. The first reason is that the company usually wants to prevent competitors from making a better product and stealing its market share and profits. The second reason is that clients who have already bought the company's product are often ready to pay much more for a slightly better product than the one they are accustomed to.

Often a company will first market a product that is only slightly better than the previous version, although a more advanced product has already been developed. Selling the products in this sequence provides a way for the company to increase profits.

When the company launches a new product, it usually does two things: It sells the new product at a higher price than that of the previous product, and it reduces by half the price of the old product. Both actions are part of a product pricing strategy, and their combination represents the theory as a whole.

A product-based company prices its products according to supply and demand, taking the competitors into consideration. Consequently, client psychology is an important factor in deciding on the price. Thus, the new product can be sold at a higher price than the previous product, because the company has already conditioned its customers to accept the cost of the older product and the benefit derived from it. Now that the company has put out a new version, which increases the benefits the client may derive from the product, the client is mentally ready to pay more for the newer product. As the company's aim is to maximize its profits, it raises the product's price to the highest level possible. At the same time, the company lowers the price of the previous product by fifty percent. Again, the reason is two-fold: The company is now interested in selling the older product to new market segments, which did not purchase the product at its initial high price. The assumption is that these same segments would similarly avoid buying the new higher priced product. If the company retained the standard price on both products, it would simply be turning its back on this segment of the market. Therefore, it is better to make a small profit than none at all. This way the company can continue selling the older product and it gains another market. Furthermore, in this way the company is able to get rid of old stock; however, this is not a pricing consideration.

Solutions-Based Companies

Let us examine the issue of pricing in a solutions-based company. Let us assume, hypothetically, that your plane has crash-landed in the middle of the desert, and you have a bag with a million dollars in cash. You are, extremely thirsty from walking under the blazing sun, when suddenly, you meet a Bedouin on a camel, carrying a flask of water. He asks for one hundred thousand dollars for the water. Wouldn't you pay for that precious bit of water? Of course you would. What good are one million dollars in cash at the moment? The water in these circumstances is worth even more. What is the real value of the water? In the tap it costs less than 10 cents, but here it is the answer to all your needs, and you'd be willing pay any price the Bedouin asks.

You probably realize that only a small portion of this story is hypothetical. It occurs repeatedly in Israeli daily life. Any time soldiers of the Israeli Defense Forces (IDF) complete an exercise in the field, whether in the mountains or in the desert, without fail the opportunist peddler shows up out of nowhere, in a kiosk on wheels, and sells the much-craved-after hot and cold beverages, ice creams and cigarettes. The soldiers refer to the peddler as "the swindler", because the prices he charges are exorbitant. The soldiers are well aware of this, but they'll buy from him nonetheless, because there is no other solution in the area. The "swindler" does not have a university degree, and even might not have graduated high school, but he is an expert at pricing. The price of the soft drink is the highest he can possibly charge while still luring the soldiers into choosing a soft drink over the water in their canteen. The "swindler" understands the solutions pricing method.

A solutions-based company charges the maximum price the customer would be willing to pay, in other words, the price is equivalent to whatever the solution is worth to the customer.

Assume you own a small business. How much do you think it costs Google to place your Internet ad so that a Web surfer that types in a key word could find your ad? The cost is minimal, but as a business owner, you might be willing to pay as much as ten dollars to have a potential customer click on your ad. The reason is simple. You have no way of estimating how much such a service should cost, and also you have no other way to advertise your business at a lower price.

Why do I bring the example of Google? Because Google has taken the notion of pricing based on value for the customer and has run with it all the way. Companies advertising with Google compete over who'll pay the highest price, and the one that does so is the winner! This method is the inverse of the tender method to which we are accustomed. Typically, in regular tenders, the suppliers offer the client the lowest price they can afford, and the buyer looks for the best offer. As you can see, in the business of supplying solutions, the situation is different. The clients understand that they have the neither the knowledge nor the ability to replace the solution provided by the supplier, and therefore they are willing to pay a price that is unrelated to the cost of the product. Clients pay whatever the product is worth to them. Thus, Google knows that there will always be those who place a high value on advertising, and opts to serve precisely those clients who are willing to pay the most.

The various pricing methods reflect the differences between manufacturing, product-based and solutions-based companies. The greater the company's knowledge leverage over the client, the freer it is to charge the highest possible prices.

When I was young, I read a story in Harvey Mackay's book, about a meeting he once had with a client. He tells that as a seller of stationary, he once met with a client and offered to sell him envelopes. The client took a pen and paper and wrote: The cost of paper in each of your envelopes is 0.1; the cost of glue is $ 0.02; the cost of printing is $ 0.05; packaging and delivery is $ 0.03; leading to a total cost of $ 0.2. You also need to make a profit so I am willing to pay 0.22 for each envelope. Mackay was shocked: The figures were accurate and therefore he had no choice but to accept the price the customer offered. Then he asked the customer how he knew the exact cost of producing an envelope, and the reply was: "My previous job for many years was to sell envelopes."

The knowledge we own is our power, and it gives us the freedom to charge almost any price we want. Knowledge is a low-value item in the company balance sheets, and the expenditure on obtaining it is far higher than its value in the books, and yet, the cost is low compared to the benefits it brings. The knowledge gap between buyer and seller is what lets us make a profit, and it motivates business owners to seek to advance from a manufacturing company to a product-based company and from there to a solutions-based company.

The following is a summary of the various pricing methods.

- Manufacturing companies calculate the direct costs, including management and overhead expenses, and add a certain percentage for profit, while the competition's prices play a major role in pricing considerations.

- Product-based companies take into consideration the statistics of supply and demand, as well as competitors' prices.

- Solutions-based companies' chief consideration is the advantage that the product affords the client.

Knowledge

Returning to the case of *Ner*, it seems that as a manufacturing company, it had no knowledge about the potential uses of the product it manufactured. It had only the knowledge required to produce the product, while the client had the advantage of knowledge related to itemized costs. Clients in fact treat manufacturing companies as a mere extension of their own ordinary production capacities. The level of knowledge and skills that a typical manufacturing company employee needs in order to complete the work task is limited and, consequently, the entire knowledge pool of manufacturing companies is poor.

During the development of a device for rescuing divers in distress called DiverGuard, I wanted to get quotes for parts from various manufacturing companies. All I had to do was send a sketch of the part required and details of the materials it should be made of. The manufacturing company did not need to know what the part was for, about the patent involved, for which industry it was intended, or what electronic parts it would contain. The manufacturing company rarely needs to understand the overall project.

Product-based companies know how their products are manufactured (often such knowledge does not come from within the company but is copied from other firms); without that knowledge they cannot function as product-based companies. Although such companies require only a very basic knowledge in order to survive, they do need extensive and innovative knowledge if they want to become a unique product company.

For example, a product-based company of a particular shampoo knows how to make shampoos, and even more sophisticated shampoos that are slightly more expensive, for people with special hair colors, or with oily hair etc. The knowledge of how to use the product remains with the client. Thus, the company is not really responsible for the use of the product according to instructions: "use a generous amount… repeat the process twice…". Shampoo companies want us to pour half a bottle when we use their products, in the hope that we'll buy more of the product. As I have never met anyone who actually uses the product according to the instructions on the package, it appears that the company does not possess knowledge about the actual use of its products; in any event, the client is unwilling to pay for such knowledge, since the company is not to be held responsible for results.

On the other hand, a company producing a patent-protected, 3-D camera has the knowledge for manufacturing and controlling the basic use of the product. As opposed to a regular product-based company, this type of camera company deals with the constant creation of knowledge. The R&D activities in the firm allow it to develop better and more expensive cameras.

Solutions-based companies pretend to know better than the clients what is good for them. The clients, for their part, are quite happy to rely on the company when choosing the particular product they need. In the solutions-based company, knowledge is not merely part of the manufacturing process, but also the major factor for which the client pays. There are also cases in which there is no physical product accompanying the knowledge. The solutions-based company is essentially a producer of knowledge, which it uses to develop new solutions and which constitutes a considerable part of the company's worth. Knowledge in the solutions-based company is an asset, and therefore the processes for creating and storing this knowledge occupy a respectable portion of the company's resources. It may even be said that the solutions-based company cannot survive long term without the ability to continually produce new knowledge.

Let us return to the example of the insurance company. As clients, we are aware that we do not know exactly what we are paying for, what the odds are that any of the scenarios in the policy may evolve, or how to compare different insurance plans. We can only hope that whatever the insurance company sells us is indeed the best solution for our needs, and that it will be there for the duration, so that in need, the solution will be viable.

In the world of Internet, the knowledge that site owners have is directly derived from observation of the use of a certain site. For example, if we use an Internet news sites to read an article that interests us, and then go back to the main page to select a new article, site owners focus on learning our preferences and trying to offer the next article that best suits our inclinations. Knowing the surfing habits of many users is immediately translated to a referral to an article that the surfing client has not even considered reading, but is exposed to due to the cumulative knowledge of the owners of the site. An excellent example of using this type of knowledge about the client is that of services that build a map of your preferences (mainly music sites).

As mentioned, knowledge is the most crucial component in the transition from a manufacturing to a product-based company, and then to a solutions-based company. The rule is:

- Manufacturing company – the client is the one in possession of knowledge and only the portion required for manufacturing is passed to the company.

- Product-based company – the knowledge for manufacturing is owned by the company, but the knowledge of the uses is owned by the clients.

- Solutions-based company – the knowledge belonging to the company is more comprehensive than the knowledge the client has, and includes also knowledge about the period during which the solution will be used.

Location

"Tell me where you live and I'll tell you who you are" – this is an adaptation of the traditional adage "tell me who your friends are, and I'll tell you who you are". The message is clear: You can learn a lot about a company by its location.

After studying manufacturing companies and observing their tendency to migrate to certain countries and not to others, I would like to shed some light on the historical processes that led to the current state of affairs.

The industrial factories in today's world are the outcome of the Industrial Revolution that took place from the mid-18th to the mid-19th centuries; particularly, the period when plants began to manufacture goods intended for use both nationally and internationally, rather than focusing solely on the closest local market. Up until the end of the 19th century, there was no such thing as workers' rights for the laborers employed in these manufacturing plants. Workers were paid the lowest possible rates, since there were always other job seekers eager to replace them, regardless of the conditions or the low wages offered. As a result, the largest manufacturing companies could be found where there was the greatest demand for jobs, namely in the richest countries of Europe as well as in the US.

The beginning of the 20th century saw the convergence of three simultaneously evolving processes, which led to the formulation of an international economic policy, which characterized the new millennium. The first process was the reduction of import taxes and tariffs on international trade. This process, which had begun in 19th century England, reached its peak by the beginning of the 20th century, when it was adopted by most of the European countries. The second process was the development of maritime transport and the building of larger and larger carriers. The third and most crucial development was the spread of the notion of the welfare state and labor laws throughout the Western world. These three processes have not stopped and are in constant evolution. Obstacles to international trade are constantly being reduced and there are many regions where free trade is the defined norm. Ships and maritime carriers are being improved to allow greater volumes, while there is a growing awareness among all countries of the need to secure the wellbeing of their citizens and workers.

As soon as states began addressing their citizens' welfare, the laborers' standard of living improved, and at the same time countries began imposing immigration restrictions, as they had no desire to increase the ranks of the lower classes and thus increase the portion of tax revenues devoted to sustaining their welfare. As a result of this change and the legislation of new labor laws, the cost of manufacturing rose significantly, and at the same time there were no more impoverished job seekers willing to replace those who demanded better conditions. This rise in production costs in the developed countries combined with the greater facility of maritime transport led to the existing situation, wherein manufacturing companies prefer to establish their factories in certain countries.

Generally speaking, product-based and solutions-based companies prefer manufacturers located in a country outside their locus of operations. The choice to outsource the manufacturing process makes sense only if it leads to significantly reduced costs. This desired outcome is unlikely if the manufacturer is in the same country, since the cost of raw materials will be the same, and in fact the manufacturer will add other elements to the cost, such as overhead and profit. Thus, outsourcing to a manufacturer in the same country inevitably means raising the price of the final product.

The only instances in which companies are likely to outsource manufacturing within the same country are if the manufacturer has the advantage of offering a unique technology and the product-based or solution-based companies do not have sufficient demand and volume of work to justify in-house manufacturing.

If the three processes described above explain the initial surge in foreign manufacturing, it is the development of the Internet that gave the definitive impetus for the more recent escalation of this tendency toward foreign manufacturing. Until the advent of the Internet, the only clients that found it economically worthwhile to handle their manufacturing needs overseas were companies with large scale production capacities, since even before the work could begin there would be the added expenditure of travelling to the destination country to explain their specific requirements. With the development of the Internet and of computer-aided design programs, the smallest of companies can find it worthwhile to order even a small number of items from a foreign manufacturer. In the Internet era, the immediacy and convenience of email and the standardization of drafting and testing programs have eliminated any pre-existing obstacles. At the same time, the cost of labor and raw materials in certain foreign countries is substantially lower, making foreign manufacturing a sure path to greater profits.

Thus, for example, while I was developing DiverGuard, I needed to order printed circuit boards. The cost of manufacturing in Israel was significantly higher than in China. Although I needed only 5 units, it was still worthwhile financially to order the work done in China and to receive high quality items within days and at an excellent price.

Product-based companies are not located where production is cheapest, but choose their location according to what is best for their marketing and development departments, where the quality (and, consequently, cost) of development is superior, and the marketing is conducted in the clients' language. Given that development and marketing are the most important parts of a product-based company, each department should be ideally located. Take Microsoft, for example: the company has development centers where there is high-quality manpower. The cost of labor is a secondary consideration. Most of Microsoft's development team is located in the US, but it also maintains an R&D center in Israel, where the cost of engineers is less than in the US, and where the people are highly creative. Microsoft's marketing is managed from the US, where most of its clients are located, but the company also has local branches in many countries. People tend to buy from those who resemble them. Therefore we prefer to shop where we have a common language with the seller. Only those who understand the local mentality can make marketing moves and sell to organizations and institutions.

As a marketing employee, I flew to many countries all over the world. I found that each place had its unique approach and different marketing emphases, which suited the local culture. The issue of the company's representation in a different country cannot be resolved by studying the language or using an automatic translator. At heart are the huge differences between the mentalities and approaches of the various societies and between the individuals of the same societies. Marketing in Germany using an Israeli approach would scare away potential clients, even if the marketing personnel were to speak German perfectly. Likewise, exhibiting a warm and relaxed attitude that is too huggy while marketing in Singapore would be interpreted as rude. I cannot even bear to imagine the scenario of a Singaporean business person being introduced to a Kazakh government minister and having to sustain a greeting of hearty hugs and sloppy kisses. If the marketing people do not speak the local mentality, they will never be able to sell.

Often product-based companies opt to keep their manufacturing in house, because the cost of labor is not a significant component in the manufacturing process compared to the need to keep proprietary knowledge from leaking to competitors. Some product-based companies may have a highly complex manufacturing process, while others need to be able to make changes during the course of manufacturing, which is often easier to do when the process is handled in house. In all these cases, the location of the manufacturing facility is less crucial, and is usually in proximity to the company's management headquarters.

In fact, there are two additional parameters that affect the location of product-based companies' manufacturing lines, namely, proximity to the supply chain and regulation. Many times, companies prefer to locate their manufacturing base close to the source of the raw materials, as in the mining of specific metals or minerals. The option of transporting large amounts of materials only to have to get rid of the remaining waste once the target material has been extracted is extremely inefficient. In cases such as these, the product company will prefer to build its manufacturing facility close to its source of supplies. The Dead Sea Works of Israel is a perfect example: Instead of transporting the water, a small portion of which contains the raw materials needed in the manufacturing process, the manufacturing facility is located on the shores of the Dead Sea, and thus has immediate access to the source materials.

In other cases, companies opt to build their manufacturing close to the customer, which has the advantage of saving on transportation expenses and the ability to both respond to and supply the customer's order on short notice. An example of this scenario is that of the Corning Company[2] which manufactures, among other things, the special glass that is used for smart phone touch screens, and especially for Apple products. Both Apple and Corning are US companies, yet the glass for Apple smart phone screens is manufactured in China.

Apple does not manufacture the products it sells. As mentioned earlier, its products are manufactured by a Chinese company called Foxconn. The Corning Company realized that it would be more cost efficient to move the glass production to China and be geographically near Foxconn, where the glass is used, rather than maintain the production site in the US and have to transport the materials to China. Not only does Corning save on transportation, but it is better able to serve its customer, Apple.

Apple is one of the most renowned examples of a product-based company that has its marketing and development headquarters located near the end customers, while the products are manufactured at various locations around the world. The Nike shoe company is another example in which

---

[2] http://www.nytimes.com/2012/01/22/business/apple-america-and-a-squeezed-middle-class.html

production is conducted at numerous locations worldwide. Both of these companies have encountered severe criticism regarding their manufacturing processes. Customers understand that while the manufacturing workers are not employed directly by the brand companies, they hold the brand companies responsible for the conditions under which the manufacturing laborers are forced to work. Customers are particularly displeased given the vast discrepancy between the enormous profits made by the brand companies and the harsh conditions under which the laborers work to produce these lucrative products. Given that these brands must preserve a positive public image, they try to persuade the manufacturers to improve the laborers' conditions, often by allocating more funds with which to pay the workers. Despite the public pressure, the brand companies refrain from taking over the manufacturing process themselves and are quite content with the current state of affairs.

In a solutions-based company, the issue of location is even more crucial. Here, not only R&D and marketing should be located in the vicinity of the client, but the company's entire supply chain should be easily accessible to customers. As mentioned, in this case, the wok of the R&D department requires familiarity with the clients' behavior in their natural environment, and a complete understanding of the client's --

not the product's-- problems. Therefore a solutions-based company cannot be located far from its clients.

One of the largest international cellular service brand names is that of Orange, a subsidiary of France Telecom. is. Orange provides cellular service to more than 35 countries across the globe. One might expect such a strong brand to exhibit and even stress the uniformity of its product, as is the case with Coca-Cola and Procter & Gamble. However, Orange understood that as a solutions-based company, it could not treat customers with varying needs in a uniform manner. Consequently, the company has established (usually through franchises) a local company in every country, which provides customers with a unique combination of products and services. Thus, for example, in African countries where customers have low-level incomes and access to electricity is irregular, the company offers low cost phones that feature a long-life battery, whereas in developed countries the company promotes high-end phones with advanced features, such as cellular Web-surfing and email access.

A solutions-based company will not survive if it cannot see eye-to-eye with the clients, and partake in their way of thinking. Clients entering a bank expect the employees to understand their verbal and non-verbal language. Hebrew-speaking clients typically would not go to an Arabic-speaking branch in Israel --even of a familiar bank, where both branches carry the same logo, because while the bank employees might speak Hebrew fluently, the Jewish, Hebrew speaking customers fear their needs might not be sufficiently understood.

In a parallel example, the arrival of Ethiopian immigrants in Israel created a gap between them and the ultimate solutions providers, namely, physicians. There were many cases in which new immigrants from Ethiopia complained of stomach aches, but as the physical examination revealed nothing out of the ordinary, the patients were sent home. Unfortunately, these visits to the doctor were often followed by incidents of suicide, murder in the family or other issues symptomatic of mental health problems. The enormous gap between the mentality of the Israeli doctor and that of the Ethiopian patient prevented the doctor from understanding that the Ethiopian patient does not usually complain of physical pain, but of mental problems and stress, and a stomach ache is the accepted way in Ethiopia to express such a complaint.

It may be claimed that only a local company, or a company with a strong local presence, can become a solutions-based company. A foreign company that wishes to penetrate a certain market must have marketing and R&D employees physically present in that market. A Chinese company that intends to sell solutions to Americans must hire people in the US or acquire a local company that will become its spearhead as a solutions supplier. You cannot provide solutions without a local presence. Apple can sell its products all over the world, but the solutions supplier providing the cellular service cannot do so from afar. Thus, when T-mobile was established in the US by Deutsche Telecom to provide solutions for the American market, the company did not even attempt to supply their solution from Germany, and when it established a presence in the US, it did not call the local company by its own name, because it was clear that its brand name had no clout in the US.

The advantage of having a local American firm is not in manufacturing, and often not even in the development of the product, but in the ability to think about the solutions Americans require. An American company cannot compete with the cost of Chinese production, or with the number of engineers in China or India. The company with a base in the US needs to take advantage of its greatest asset, namely, its location. The advantage of location cannot be based on protective customs rates or the cost of importing goods from China, but on the company's ability to understand the American customer in the largest market in the world, in a way that no one else can.

To summarize,

- Manufacturing companies – can be located anywhere in the world where there are advantages of cost, in terms of labor, premises, or similar advantages.

- Product-based companies – should have the R&D and marketing departments located in the clients' market, so as to understand the nature of the market for which their products are intended. The manufacturing and management divisions needn't be located close to the customers.

- Solutions-based companies –must have the entire company located near the clients, because on the one hand, the customers expect that their needs and their way of thinking will be completely clear and obvious to the company, and on the other hand, in order to meet this expectation, the R&D staff needs to be able to the interact directly with the customers.

The theory global effect

Addressing a single problem with a single answer provides a solution. Addressing two problems with a single answer creates a theory.

We have the privilege of living in interesting times: Entire processes can be completed from start to finish in no more than a flash; a task that a thousand years ago might have taken decades, and a hundred years ago took several years, can now be accomplished in a matter of days. Empires rise and fall with enormous speed, companies can reach a market value equivalent to that of an entire country within a few years, and a letter is transmitted from one end of the globe to the other in a few seconds. This state of affairs dictates the need to conduct faster analyses and to create simpler theories and solutions, if we wish to cope successfully with the rapid pace of the world we live in.

Nowadays, the two global superpowers face two different -- perhaps even opposing--difficulties. In the East, China is facing the results of a history of manufacturing-based economy, while in the West, the US is coping with a manufacturing sector that is dwindling at a worrying pace.

In China, the problem arose as a result of the increase in the standard of living of hundreds of millions of Chinese citizens, which came in response to production plant employees' rising demands for improved social conditions. This in turn led to the erosion of China's competitive edge in manufacturing. Some companies have already transferred their production lines from China to countries that feature a lower standard of living, such as Vietnam and Cambodia.

In the US, due to high production costs, most companies opted to move their manufacturing facilities to China or to other countries with a similarly low cost of living; consequently, the country is now facing high unemployment rates, especially among the uneducated population, as there is virtually no call for manual labor.

As often happens, each party holds the solution to the other's problem…

Let us start with the problem which seems to beg for a seemingly obvious solution, namely, the Chinese problem.

The Chinese government is trying to encourage companies in China to transition from the manufacturing of products intended for foreign labels to the development and marketing of their own products, as a way of increasing profit margins, which would lead to higher salaries and thus minimize the country's dependence on production plants. There is nothing essentially new about this approach, which has been adopted and implemented on numerous occasions; however, the point underscored here is that there's nothing simple about building a company that functions in the American model. A company can't just suddenly decide to shift gears and switch from manufacturing items for an American company to manufacturing and marketing its own --albeit similar-- products. In fact, many companies in China attempted to make this change and failed. This shift requires the company to alter its perspective, from manufacturing to product management, and as a product-based company, its tasks will differ substantially from those of a manufacturing company. Not sure? Good! Because that's what this book is for: To find out what it takes for a company to shift from a manufacturing focus to a product focus and from there on to the more sophisticated target of becoming a solutions-based company.

The solution to the American problem is in China. I know this may sound like a contradiction in terms, but let's consider the process in China and see what the Americans need to learn from the Chinese in order to solve their unemployment problem and how solving the Chinese problem will help the Americans address their problem. In the 1980s, a vast production sector that had developed over several decades in the US reached its peak. Up until that point in time, American companies traditionally had employed numerous production workers, and the entire manufacturing process, from start to finish, was managed in-house. Of course, this meant that companies had to have expertise in many fields, instead of focusing solely on what they did best. This diffused focus led to inefficiency in many processes, and gradually these processes were outsourced. Outsource companies specializing in particular activities began replacing the inefficient departments of larger companies. However, this change did not lead to mass unemployment, luckily, since most of the workers who had been dismissed from the larger companies were then employed by the newly established expert companies. Despite outsourcing some parts of the manufacturing process, a significant portion of the work continued to take place in-house, so that production was not completely divorced from the parent company.

The next stage that evolved was the improvement of production quality in the East. This intensified the competition among manufacturing companies vying for large companies' projects, as more contenders entered into what became an international arena, where low cost labor ruled the playing field. Many specialized American companies were forced to close down, and most of the manufacturing of American product components was moved to China. Inevitably, the next logical step for American companies then was to move also the assembly of these imported parts to the East, until finally, the few US manufacturers that remained had no choice but to join the relocation trend. As a result, the number of blue collar jobs available in the US has been in constant decline.

Up until this point, we've followed the evolution of the problem in the US; now let's turn to the solution. There are two parts to this solution, and while they are not interdependent, both are necessary, if a full-fledged solution is to be attained.

The first part, to risk sounding simplistic, is the establishment of manufacturing companies in the USA, using the manufacturing advantages available to the US. You're probably asking yourself now "what advantages, precisely, does the US have in terms of manufacturing, compared to China?" You may be surprised, but further on in this book you'll discover that a manufacturing company relies not only on its laborers, but also on other factors, such as supply schedules, performance levels and accountability. In regard to all business aspects that lie beyond the actual cost of manufacturing, geographical proximity to the customer and a shared mind-set constitute an indisputable advantage, which gives North American manufacturers a viable position in the market. Unfortunately, many Americans have forgotten what it means to be a manufacturing company. Those who have tried to establish such a company have found either that their marketing and sales representatives tend to address the customers using the lingo of product-based companies, or they themselves have opted for the standard American company structure, which is unsuitable for the type of lean and nimble operations that a manufacturing company requires. In other words, anyone who wishes to establish or promote a manufacturing company in the US would have to rediscover the recently forgotten formula for functioning as a manufacturing company.

The second component of the solution to the US problem depends on China. As the number of Chinese companies transitioning from manufacturing to product management increases, the price of Chinese imports will rise in tandem, making it increasingly easier for US manufacturers to compete in the local market. As will be demonstrated at a later point, the price of a product issued by a product-based company is by definition higher than that of a product that comes from a manufacturing company. Therefore, the rise in the standard of living in China and the emergence of companies with a wider profit margin can be expected to erode the Chinese advantage of low production costs and create a more even playing field in the competition between US and Chinese businesses. Eventually, some of the American industrialized manufacturers will be able to compete with the labor-intensive Chinese companies even within China.

Operations Management

For each company, there is a basic phase in which the company creates the value for which the customer pays. Managing this stage is known as operations management, since it operates the center of the business. Operations management may be the independent management of a professional, such as a barber or a tailor, or it may refer to the management of hundreds of thousands of employees in numerous plants. In each case, an operation is at the heart of the company's activities, and therefore it is completely different in nature for manufacturing, product-based or solutions-based companies.

Manufacturing Companies

To understand the role of operations manager in a manufacturing company, I chose the example of Ken (pseudonym), vice president of operations in a machine tools company, which provides its customers with machine-tooling services based on the customers' diagrams. In his previous role, Ken managed the engineering department of the company, and had been promoted to this role three years earlier. His main responsibility now was to see that all machines in the company were working smoothly. In order to do his job to the best possible level, he attended to proper maintenance of the machines, managed troubleshooting and saw to it that the next job was lined up as soon as a machine became available. The latter meant avoiding lags from the engineering department, which is responsible for getting the drawings and instructions from the customers and making sure that all details are covered and the job is ready to go to production.

Over the last year, Ken managed to increase output by 12%. This achievement enabled quicker supply of customer orders, resulting in increased profitability for the company. I asked Ken how he managed to increase production at such an impressive rate.

The secret lies in the relations between engineering and production. Only after I moved to production did I understand that the first-in-first-out (FIFO) method we'd been using in the engineering department might be fair to the client, but was highly inefficient for the company. Sometimes we'd get two orders, with very little difference between them, which would require using the same tools for production. At engineering, we weren't aware of the time it takes to setup each machine. Only when I started my work here did I realize that it made more sense to do the similar jobs sequentially, so as not to have to set up the same machines twice. Once I saw how much time was wasted preparing the machines, I implemented a work method that would reduce to a minimum the time spent on setting up. Under this method, engineering had to take on another, relatively marginal role, which was to sort and arrange incoming orders by machine, effectively reducing time spent on operations setup. This is how I managed to get 12% more production from the same machines.

Product-Based Companies

In a product-based company, as compared to a manufacturing company, the operations manager has more responsibility. The role entails managing processes and interfaces between various groups, where coordination consumes a lot of expensive management time. For example, a company manufacturing communication cables has departments producing copper cables, others that coat the cables, and next the cable roll is passed to another department that binds several coated cables together and provides external coating, resistant to environmental conditions. Then the cables are passed on for cutting to the desired length, and mounted on communication fixtures. Finally, the cables are packaged in bags and the bags are packed in crates and prepared for delivery. When an order arrives, the operations manager must prepare the entire process, which involves coordinating the operations of a large number of departments and ensuring each stage of the job is synchronized with the next, so that the product can be supplied on time, based on the company's commitment to the client.

An additional responsibility of the operations manager in a manufacturing company is to document not only the manufacturing process pertaining to each of the company's product, but also to document each of the processes designed per order. The purpose of the documentation is to enable the precise reconstruction of the previous supply order for the same customer, and also to identify a point of failure in case the order was not supplied properly. To recall, the operations manager in a manufacturing company, in contrast, has no need to reconstruct the production process, but only oversees how the employees perform their jobs.

Solutions-Based Companies

The operations manager in a solutions-based company has additional responsibility, namely, to ensure that the product is used properly by the client. Given that it is the company that has the knowledge of how to use the product, and often it installs the product for the client, the operations manager is responsible also for this final stage of the product's life, training clients and assimilating solutions for them, or operating the teams that actually run the product for the client. For example, a company that provides highly sophisticated software usually sends employees to the client's premises to make sure the client receives a perfect solution. To this end, the company employs assimilators, whose job it is to explain to the client how to use the software, and also service and support personnel, who make sure the software continues to run properly.

To summarize, the role of the operations manager in a

- Manufacturing company – is to improve the functioning and make processes more efficient.

- Product-based company – to coordinate the phases of the production process and manage documentation

- Solutions-based company – in addition to overseeing production, there is also field work such as installation and training.

Documentation

In the previous chapter, I mentioned the issue of documentation as part of the responsibility of the operations manager. Here I would like to raise the importance of documentation, and the documentation requirements that are pertinent to each of the company types.

In a manufacturing company, there is hardly any need to document the work. Once work on the customer-supplied drawing is completed, it is approved and filed in archives in case clarifications are sought or a customer's claims need to be examined. In a sense, the documentation of a manufacturing company's work is done by the client, who owns the knowledge of what to produce, and the specifications for doing so.

In a product-based company, documentation is far more crucial and complex. While I was working for *Feb*, I had to demonstrate a product to a person of influence in a country whose market it was important for us to penetrate. The demonstration was scheduled at the last moment and therefore I pressed the manufacturing department to prepare everything within two days, to have it packed and ready for me to take on the flight. The manufacturing department cooperated and the product was ready on time. When I came to the client with the product and wanted to demonstrate how it worked, I saw that one of its main functions, which was the reason we persuaded the client to meet with us in the first place, was not operational. I apologized profoundly and promised to have a working specimen flown in from Israel by the next day. That night I had an employee fly over with an alternative product, which was not exactly what the client wanted, but had the missing function. After three flights and long waits in two different airports, the employee came with the product, and the demonstration was reasonable. Of course, if the function had been operational in the first place, the client's overall impression would have been better. When I returned, we gathered the manufacturing personnel and tried to figure out what went wrong with the first specimen. Clearly, this failure, which had severe repercussions, including an inferior demonstration and tens of thousands of dollars to cover the flight of the other employee, had to be identified and dealt with. We found out from the documentation of the manufacturing process, that deviating from protocol, one department had conducted its portion of the production before another department. This departure from the correct procedure, which occurred because of time constraints, was the reason for the product's malfunctioning. The conclusion was, of course, that the order of operations must never be changed. Without the precise documentation of the process, including time of admission of the product to each department and the work done there, we would not have been able to trace the problem and eliminate potential repeats.

We therefore see that the scope of documentation in a product-based company is much greater than in a manufacturing company. Given that the company is responsible for all of the product's functionalities, it is vital that it document precisely the work processes, so as to be able to reconstruct them when necessary. In addition, documentation helps the pricing process, as it allows us to assess the time and materials each department has invested in the product.

For an example of a solutions-based company, let's consider documentation in a public transportation system. Each day, many parameters need to be documented, from the number of passengers to the weather conditions. The data allow the company to determine whether additional buses/trains will be needed on a particular day. Thus, the fact that the company needs to monitor its products and ensure their operation in any environment and at any given time requires that the work be documented, not only during production but even after sales. In this case, the documentation does not relate to the product's functionalities, which remain constant from one day to the next, but rather to the trends of use, such as the increase in the number of commuters on rainy days and changes in congestion following the opening of new roads. Determining the trends of use must include also an in-depth segmentation of the market.

An additional example of documentation in a solutions-based company may be seen in the *Soluto*[3] company. One of the latest trends is the use of common knowledge for solving problems. A company that does this successfully is Soluto: Its software program enables any computer owner to decide which programs to run. It provides the user with statistical data (gathered from other *Soluto* users) pertinent to the programs that are being run on the user's PC. Based on

---

[3] https://www.soluto.com/

this information the user can understand the relative importance of each of the programs currently running and can decide whether it is necessary. As the example of *Soluto* clearly demonstrates, the distinguishing factor in a solutions-based company, which gives the company its relative advantage on the market, is the information it has gathered and its and documentation of this information.

To summarize, in

- Manufacturing companies – there is hardly any need for documentation, because usually the client documents the data required for completing the product.

- Product-based companies – documentation of production processes and costs is required in order to enable reconstruction and pricing of the product, and also in order to improve it.

- Solutions-based companies – documentation is required not only for production, but also to monitor product behavior and its effect in the field.

The Company Employees

As I have already told you, I began working for *Feb* while the company was undergoing a process of internal change. The company owners knew that this move should be accompanied by the recruitment of new personnel. The company recruited R&D people to develop new products, as well as new marketing people. Recruiting R&D people to develop new products was self-evident, but I have often come upon companies that did not understand that a transition to a more sophisticated product was best accompanied by the recruitment of a new cadre of marketing people. Marketing a technologically smart product requires a certain level of expertise, in order to explain to the clients why such a product is better than the one they are used. Marketers who do not understand the ins and outs of the product will have a hard time making the sale.

Returning to the case of *Ner*, we find that 85% of its employees work on the production line. Since a manufacturing company usually has a limited number of clients and a lot of production work, a small management and financial staff and a few sales people can suffice to maintain the company.

Salaries in a manufacturing company are usually lower than the average in the market, since the key to the existence of a manufacturer is the ability to produce cheaply. Nevertheless, the cost of labor is the main component in the product's sale price. This leads to constant tension within the company, and the attempt of managers to reduce production costs by lowering wages. In the best case scenario, reducing or not raising wages leads to frustration and high turnover of personnel.

The rule is that the cost of replacing an employee increases with the increased training period. In a manufacturing company, the cost of training people is low and therefore company owners do not go out of their way to avoid turnover. In addition, most employees in a manufacturing company have no contact with the clients; thus, since the company owners don't need the employees to market the organization favorably, they have no particular interest in keeping their employees satisfied.

My neighbor was looking for a part time evening job during his high-school studies, and found work as a waiter for a catering company. His training consisted of the following: "come tomorrow at six wearing a white shirt". During the evening he distributed food to the tables and cleared dirty dishes. Unfortunately, during the evening, he dropped a tray with steaming stew on the table. You can imagine the state of the guests and his continued apologies. It was his last evening in this profession, and no one regretted his leaving. Here's an alternative scenario: I read an interview with a waiter who has held the same job in a three-star Michelin restaurant for 35 years and claims he's enjoyed every minute. He has become part of the restaurant's reputation, and his retirement will be a hard blow to the owners.

The difference between that catering company and the 3-star Michelin restaurant represents the difference between a manufacturing and a product-based company. In product-based companies, we find R&D departments with several documentation people. In addition, they also have a marketing department in charge of building the company brand and introducing the products to clients under the company logo. In product-based companies, the number of production employees is usually smaller than in a manufacturing company, and sometimes non-existent, as the actual manufacturing is often outsourced. In such cases, the company employs only a minimal number of people to maintain its ongoing operations, but the actual product that the client pays for is produced elsewhere.

The level of expertise required of workers in product-based companies is higher than that required in manufacturing companies; therefore, their salaries are higher. However, since the company sells not only production capacity but also knowledge, the percentage of labor cost in the product's end price is lower than it is in manufacturing companies.

Employee turnover is significantly lower in product-based companies, as seen in the example of the waiter in the Michelin restaurant. Employees of product-based companies are often aware that they have to keep commercial secrets from reaching the competition. In addition, the workers acquire various skills; hence turnover costs are relatively high.

Many product-based companies fear for their brand name, and know that a disgruntled employee may cause grave damage to their image. Therefore, even if employees are let go, their way out is padded with many benefits, to avoid any damage to the company's reputation after their departure. To keep employees from frequently quitting the company, employee conservation plays an important role in the human resources (HR) department, while in manufacturing companies the HR is responsible mainly for hiring and firing.

There are numerous examples of the efforts to conserve employees, some you know of personally and others by rumor. Such a balance of powers was only a dream for employees a hundred years ago, and even today it is not common among workers in a manufacturing company. For example, Intel gives it employees a few months of sabbatical leave, and other perks, such as reduced priced tickets to concerts and parks. Other companies give valuable gifts for the holidays or at the end of the year, in order to enhance the employee's emotional commitment to the firm, and thus minimize turnover.

In a solutions-based company we shall find the best R&D and marketing people available, and they are far more knowledgeable than the client. The solutions-based company treats its employees as its most valuable asset, because without them and their knowledge, the company would lose its position on the market as a solutions-based company, and revert to being one of many product companies.

Conservation of knowledge in the solutions-based company is a major component in the company's assets. An employee who leaves the company takes with her all the knowledge acquired on the job, knowledge which the company needs if it is to develop new products and ensure its future. Even in companies in which knowledge is constantly documented, there's no replacement for the specific knowledge that each employee possesses. Employees in a solutions-based company should be proud of their place of work and are expected to contribute to its development over time. Therefore, it is the company's mission to make the employees proud of it by means of concrete incentives, such as gifts and bonuses or by more encompassing acts such as promotions.

The solutions-based company also employs field people, assimilators, field researchers, demonstrators and installers, whose role is to present the client with the complete solution. Manufacturing and product-based companies do not have such positions to offer, and usually rely on specialized sub-contractors to fulfill these functions. In contrast to the former two, if a solutions-based company uses sub-contractors, it remains, nonetheless, responsible also for the result of the work of the field personnel. It will therefore employ people to supervise the sub-contractors' work, to make sure that the end result in the field meets its standards. Let us take an example from the hospitality industry. The role of the hotel is to provide clients with a room, but it also provides a total service experience, which may be defined as a solution. In many hotels, the cleaning personnel are not hotel employees but sub-contracted though a cleaning company; however, since the hotel is responsible towards the customers, it employs a supervisor to check on the cleaning personnel and make sure they do their jobs properly.

Naturally, in a solutions-based that emphasizes a long-term global vision; management will opt to deal less with the production aspects and more with processes and strategic directions. One may think occasionally that some of the management team is disconnected from the company's daily activities and therefore should be considered superfluous, a waste of precious resources; in truth, such thinking may hinder the continued development of the company as a solutions-based company. To remain solutions-based, a company should always be one step ahead of its clients, and thus will always employ people to examine the medium-range and the long-term goals and plans.

Employees of a solutions-based company are the firm's display window, as they maintain the relationship with the client. A solutions-based company therefore cannot afford to have a dissatisfied employee, since the information that such a disgruntled employee might let slip in a moment of anger has the potential to cause the company grave damage. Every employee who leaves a solutions-based company causes some damage, and the company strives to minimize this damage, by maintaining good relations (contractual and non-contractual) with those who have left. An employee who continues to support the company even after he has left it gives the company the stability it requires in order to continue to create new solutions. To maintain such good relations, the employee is usually given generous benefits, which make him grateful to the company and ready to assist it in any way.

Google is currently a good example of a solutions-based company. Google started as a company providing solutions for finding useful and up-to-date information on the Internet. Although it seems as though the company sells a product, namely, the relevant search results for what the surfer seeks, in fact it is a solutions-based company. What Google provides is not the information of the search, but the ability to search and find the most pertinent and current information, and as the user gets these consistently over time, it becomes increasingly obvious that Google knows what it is doing and its solution is reliable. Google's solutions are long-term and, therefore, a one-off sale would be meaningless. Consequently, Google nurtures its employees so that they are reluctant to leave the company, because anyone who leaves damages the human knowledge base accumulated in the firm.

To summarize, the significance of the role played by company employees varies according to the category of the type of business at hand: In

- Manufacturing companies– most employees work in production and are treated as a resource. Their knowledge or opinion about their work place is not very relevant and no effort is made to keep them aboard. The manufacturing company employs a limited number of management, financial and marketing personnel.

- Product-based companies– employ, in addition to production workers, professional R&D and documentation personnel. The knowledge necessary for production comes from within the company; therefore, there is a need to keep the employees from leaving the company. It is important that employees with this knowledge do not transfer to the competition. The marketing in the company becomes more professional compared to that of a manufacturing company.

- Solutions-based companies – employ R&D experts in the relevant fields. They are joined by field workers, and the level of marketing is even more professional. The company employees are its most important asset and therefore their conditions are constantly improved and great effort is expended to prevent them from leaving. The management deals with long-term processes rather than with issues related to production and manufacturing.

Sales

Every company sells its clients something for money or money's worth. The product changes from one company to another. It may be something tangible like gold ingots, or something as abstract as an idea. In some cases, the value that the client gets is immediately apparent. For example, a client of a soft drink company would assess the value of the purchase by its ability to quench thirst, and by the degree to which the flavor was pleasing. In contrast, a weather forecasting company provides something that the client values, even though it is often not what was promised. The common denominator for all things sold by companies is that someone is willing to pay for them.

As mentioned in the first chapter, the portion of the customer's payment that pertains to tangible assets varies from company to company (sometimes this percentage equals 0%). The governing rule is that the greater the portion of intangible assets in a sale, the higher the percentage of gross profit from that sale. There are thousands of examples, worldwide. The percentage of gross profit on tickets to a football game is much lower than that gained from selling the rights to broadcast the same game on television. The percentage of profit from selling a given product is significantly lower than from selling the rights to use a certain technology. We shall see that as the company shifts from selling manufacturing capacities to selling products, and then to selling solutions, the percentage of tangible assets becomes smaller, while the percentage of gross profit rises. In a manufacturing company, the main part the client pays for is the cost of labor and raw materials. The client pays for valuables that can be seen and felt. Manufacturing companies operate in a competitive market, where their advantage for the client focuses on low labor costs as a result of geographic location, or as a result of the advantage of size and the volume of work done. In addition, the manufacturing company charges for the storage of the raw materials it owns, and the benefit for the client is in not having to purchase wholesale quantities of raw materials and remain with unused stock.

In a product-based company, the company sells its knowledge on how to produce a certain product, as well as the hours invested in bringing the product on the market. In addition, the company sells the image for the user of the product, embodied in the brand in which the company invests. For example Rolex sells the client a high quality watch in which many hours of development have been invested, but the main thing the client pays for is not the tangible watch, but rather the company nurtured image of the type of people who use the watches it has developed. In coming to purchase this product, the client is aware of paying for the image, because there are plenty of cheaper options for a product that tells time.

In a solutions-based company, the major component in the sale is the knowledge of how to solve the client's problem, and the value for the client stems from using and owning this solution. The confidence that this problem no longer needs to be attended to is worth far more to the client than the sum price of the solution's tangible components. Typically, the client of a solutions-based company finds it difficult to estimate the company's expenses and compare these with the price set for the solution, but this is no deterrent to actually making the purchase! In the case of a solutions-based company, the client pays for the availability of the solution as part of the product. A client buying a subscription for a service that alerts him of police speed traps expects the service to operate as and when required, regardless of the amount of time her car is on the road. The main part of the sale is intangible and, therefore, as mentioned, the pricing on a solutions-based purchase is very different from the pricing considerations in other company types.

To summarize:

- Manufacturing companies sell labor, storage and the purchase of materials.

- Product-based companies sell the knowledge of how to produce the product, in addition to production costs.

- Solutions-based companies sell the knowledge of how to solve the client's problems, in addition to the product.

Research &Development

A company that belongs to one of my best friends, and sells mainly to the military market, decided to upgrade from a manufacturing company to a product-based company. In its current status, the company did not have qualified people on board who could define and develop new products, so it contacted and successfully recruited the two most notable experts in the IDF. This created an astounding effect, whereby the company's main client, the IDF, contained the knowledge center, but the people who characterized and drew the products had shifted their alliance to the company, which was now both the designer and the manufacturer. No one remained in the IDF to characterize the products, and it did not have the necessary specifications to request price quotes for these products. As a result, the company began to receive requests from its clients for solutions to problems; thus, it turned out that it had to make a direct switch from being a manufacturing company to a solutions-based company. Although the company still had to make additional changes (some of which have been implemented already), the most significant change that altered its status was the establishment of an R&D department, and the recruitment of the best specialists to staff it.

One of the things by which to determine if a company is a product- or a solutions-based company is the R&D department.

A manufacturing company hardly needs R&D. It receives all the information required for production from the clients; therefore, the only R&D required relates to the improvement of processes within the company. If there are engineers in the company, they deal with in-house improvements of machinery and work processes. These employees are mainly industrial and management engineers.

The product-based company invests in R&D to improve its products. The engineers usually focus on improving previous versions of products, upgrading them to newer models. The R&D department is the key to implementing a status shift from a manufacturing to a product-based company. A well-established R&D department is a necessary investment if the company goal is to continue to thrive.

The R&D department is responsible also for the development of new products, which are synergistically compatible with the company's infrastructure. The synergy may be compatible with the company's manufacturing capabilities (a new product manufactured in-house) or with the company's market niche (new product for existing clientele).

For example, Nokia tries to back to her position as a market leader in the cellular devices market. In order to do so Nokia invested 4.782 billion Euros, which represented 15.8% of Nokia net sales in 2012[4]. A product-based company must improve its products, as mentioned in the chapter on pricing, because if it does not launch new products, its competitors will do so. And that's exactly what happened to Nokia, after having been the market leader for years with more than 50% of the market; she lost her leadership and her brand value to Apple and Samsung which came with "smartphones" when Nokia was late to this game.

---

[4] http://i.nokia.com/blob/view/-/2246090/data/2/-/form20-f-12-pdf.pdf

In the solutions-based company, the expenditure on R&D is divided differently than in a product-based company. The solution company needs to know its clients better than they know themselves. Therefore, a large part of its research is not focused on its current products, as is done in product-based companies, but is invested in searching for problems that the clients might encounter, even before they are aware of them. The solutions-based company involves strategic clients in characterizing the solutions needed, by using focus groups or through daily contact with the client. With the help of these sources, the company can determine the problems, and study their behavior. In addition, the solutions-based company always seeks multi-disciplinary solutions, because these can provide a more comprehensive and inclusive solution, which in turn can increase the company's income and profit.

For example, the solutions supplier, Google, spends over 13%[5] of its sales revenue on R&D. Although users do not necessarily request more innovative solutions, the company is constantly working to improve its products. In this manner, by ensuring that customers consistently find in

---

[5] http://investor.google.com/financial/tables.html

Google the best solution to their needs, it gains the customers' trust.

In a solutions-based company, it is difficult to predict which of the company's newly developed products and technologies will be adopted by the clients. Therefore, the company is aware that a large part of the R&D expenditure is invested in developing products that will never reach the market. Solutions-based companies operate in a market in which the clients are not yet aware of either their own needs or of the solutions they are about to receive; by definition then, the company cannot be completely certain how new products will be received. Companies cannot ask the customer to evaluate the solution before it is placed on the market, and even if it were possible to question customers directly, the customers' ability to forecast their response to new technologies is limited, at best. Typically, customers know how much money they are prepared to invest for the purchase of either a more advanced model of a particular product they are currently using or a different product with clearly defined advantages. However, they find it much more difficult to assess in advance their attitude towards a new form of solution. For example, before the launch of the Internet, customers could never have imagined its effect on their lives. Nevertheless it is currently standard practice to have vast amounts of knowledge freely available and accessible at home as well as to read opinions of and communicate with people from all over the world in a matter of seconds. Every technological revolution has been accompanied by doubters, those who could not see the potential benefits they stood to gain from its use. The introduction of the first cars on the market was accompanied by demonstrations held by the carriage owners, who claimed that the new vehicles were scaring the horses and constituted a danger to pedestrians. Many failed to recognize the change that cars would bring to the world.

In cellular communications companies, for example, R&D efforts involve a constant search for usage packages, which will induce customers to commit for longer periods, remain loyal and spend more money. One of the developments in the field of cellular companies was the Multimedia Messaging Service, or MMS, the ability to send messages that include multimedia content. Unlike many other services, this service failed to draw a large number of users, and the cellular companies stopped marketing it aggressively. Before the MMS service was developed, we did not think we would need it, and even after its development, customers did not look for it on their phones. This is an example of a product which was developed in a solutions company, but failed to take off. By contrast, cellular Internet services have become a considerable source of income for these companies. Who would have predicted a few years ago that we would be willing to pay so much to be able to access the Internet from anywhere?

The example of one of the biggest toys companies in the world attempt to conduct part of their R&D processes directly with customers highlights the importance and uniqueness of development methods in a solutions-based company. This company develops toys and games; therefore, the decision to test potential products meant gathering a group of children, exposing them to a large number of new toys and games, and letting them play freely, to their hearts' content. The games the children liked most were manufactured and distributed in toy stores. The products failed miserably in the market, despite the tests conducted with the children's focus group. Also products designated for production and marketing based on a second focus group failed. The internal investigation conducted by the company revealed the following flaw: all of the games the children played with were entirely new to them; there was no opportunity for them to choose between familiar toys and the brand new ones. However, in the real test ground, that is, at the store, the children preferred the good old games.

The company failure emphasizes the differences between R&D in product- and in solutions-based companies. In the former, the firm strives to improve products and invent new ones, and the process is conducted within the company. In a solutions-based firm, R&D is conducted at the client's, to determine the problems in the field. Had the company chosen to spend several hours observing children at play in their regular environments, they would have gained greater insights.

I occasionally read about company managers who go into the field, in order to analyze the clients' behavior in their own territory. In one particular case, managers of a TV station in Israel went to customers' homes and spent several hours collecting information on the customers' viewing habits. The managers were very proud of their decision to conduct field observations. This exercise failed, and the reasons became apparent upon reading the article: it was bad enough that this was a one-time event instead of part of an ongoing effort, but having this excursion led by senior management instead of by professional R&D staff made it worse, since it meant that their goal was merely to form a very general impression and a one-off understanding. A company that supposedly aims to provide a rich viewing experience and an overall family entertainment solution, but fails to investigate customers' viewing behaviors at home regularly is bound to miss the mark.

The solutions-based company has a group of clients that represents the variety of its customers, and it is with this group that the company conducts its research. Given that the company constantly needs to remain at the forefront of technology, it seeks and documents clients' feedback regarding every type of usage or service provided, in an attempt to understand the clients better than they understand themselves.

Israel is ranked as the fourth exporter of arms in the world. Taking into consideration the fact that there are fewer people in Israel than in some cities of the world and sixty years ago not a single company could manufacture military equipment legally, this fact requires examination.

Hearing about the scope of military equipment exported brings to mind the incessant disputes between Israel and its neighbors, and the number of wars Israel was involved in. It is a common belief that Israel's ability to produce high-quality weapons and sell them in large quantities all over the world was born of necessity: Israel had to produce military equipment in order to survive.

Although this statement may ring true, it provides neither an adequate nor an accurate explanation of this phenomenon. Indeed, the simple facts show that there are many countries that have been involved in the same number of wars (for example, Israel's adversaries in those wars) or even more. As I see it, there are a number of factors, which often escape our attention, that contribute to and explain the success of Israel's military equipment industries. Due to these factors, Israel is nearly the sole solutions provider in this market, while all the other military equipment suppliers are product-based companies. The factors described here are inter-dependent, and show the Israeli military equipment industry in a different light.

The first factor that can explain the success of Israel military equipment companies is the fact that they view themselves as solutions providers and not as product suppliers. The reason for this could be found in Israeli companies' R&D culture, which is informal and includes the clients throughout the process, the client is IDF and its various units. By default, the development and marketing experts in the Israeli company have been through military service, so when they want to test the developed product, they ask a "favor" from their army buddies. Such favors, which can mean conducting flights or operating entire units, provide the foundation on which the Israeli R&D culture thrives. These tests are typically coordinated between the company and the officers in the field, without involving senior command levels or any other formal authorizing entities in the military. This open culture means that any soldier in the field can address and congratulate the company's general manager who is there to observe the test, and openly express an opinion or offer suggestions on how the product might be improved. Nowhere else in the world is the process so informal and open. I myself have visited many military facilities in the world in my capacity as marketing manager, and every time I demonstrated a product or tried to understand the client's needs or desires, I met with restrained military courtesy: "the product is impressive", "thank you for coming", "we have learned a lot", or "we shall certainly try to purchase it". Only in the IDF have I managed to receive constructive comments, such as "What makes you think I could carry this on my back?" "There's no way we're going to use this", "it is too difficult to maneuver", and other comments that reveal what the customer truly thinks.

Also other agents from around the world who were affiliated with the company in which I worked claimed that they never received useful feedback. The reason that I could obtain such real feedback from the IDF was not because I'm Israeli, but because the potential customers in this case were Israeli soldiers. In other countries, professional soldiers in professional armies work by the book rather than as members of their supplier's development team.

The first time we encounter Israeli "chutzpah" and its consequences is in the Bible. The Bible tells of Pharaoh, King of Egypt, who is unable to solve a dream he had. Joseph, the slave imprisoned in Egypt, is called upon to decipher the meaning of the dream. He does so; however, without being asked, he solves not only the mystery of the dream's meaning, but also the problem predicted by the dream, as he provides a detailed operational plan for a solution. The courage he demonstrates in ignoring the class differences and facing the king directly, as well as his instructions for solving the problem impress the Pharaoh, who adopts the program devised. I personally know a large number of soldiers and officers who addressed a company's CEO directly and described their own vision of how the product being developed should behave. Upon completing their military service, these individuals found their way to the R&D department of that same firm. Here we begin to understand one of the main factors that contribute to Israeli companies' success in the global military industry market: its R&D department includes the clients in the development in ways unparalleled anywhere else.

A second component in the success of Israeli companies is the cultural axiom that states "of course we can". Another aspect of this cultural phenomenon is the "you can count on me" approach, which effectively means "don't worry, everything will be OK --and don't expect me to give you a detailed account of how we'll get there". This attitude has often led to problems and severe dysfunctions, and other times it has led to unbridled success. Here too, the roots of this attitude can be found in the Bible, which includes numerous stories demonstrating the victory of few against many, while ignoring stories of defeat in similar circumstances. These biblical stories create a sense of empowerment, of defying normative boundaries. The interpreted message is "you can do it", "where there's a will there's a way'. People involved in field marketing share this culture, so that when the client asks that the product perform an additional function, they respond "no problem, trust me". In fact, forcing the R&D people to deal with the promises made by the marketers makes them more creative and, as a result, they often supply a more comprehensive solution. In addition, marketing people know that in a pinch, Israeli culture allows them to include products of another company as part of their package, with the confidence that the other company will be willing to include its products in the same package. Thus, instead of just selling the product they produce, they sell the client a complete solution.

To summarize, different R&D departments have a different focus, depending on the type of company.

- Manufacturing companies– focus on improving production processes.

- Product-based companies – focus on developing and improving existing products or on responding to a client's request.

- Solutions-based companies– focus on cooperating with strategic clients to understand their problems and develop multi-disciplinary products.

Marketing

Remember why I started writing this book? It was because of marketing. How do you market a manufacturing company? The truth is I do not have a complete answer, but I believe that together we can think of a formula that will give us some idea.

I have come across numerous manufacturing companies in my line of work, and since I strive to be helpful even when no immediate compensation is involved, I'm always happy to recommend good companies in the market. I've often wondered what to say when I give a recommendation. I could describe what the company produced for me, but this information might not be relevant to this potential client in particular. I can't talk about its abilities, because I know only the aspects related to the project it completed for me. Therefore when recommending a manufacturing company, I always talk about the people, how thorough and efficient they are, their ability to make and adapt any product per my order, and their adherence to the time schedule agreed upon. In addition, I tell about the level and range of their prices, and the return for value. So my typical recommendation of a manufacturing company may sound like this: "If you need a assembly company, you should work with X; the people are wonderful, whenever I call, they're always remarkably patient and helpful. They have the most advanced equipment and there is nothing they can't do. And the price? Excellent. If I'd wanted to produce this by myself, it would have cost me double." Now let me ask you: Is this marketing?

Of course this isn't the type of activity a marketing department undertakes, yet most manufacturing companies do not have a marketing department. Their marketing consists of sales people whose role is to maintain contact with the clients, and make sure that the next time the client will be ready for a manufacturing project; this client will inevitably choose to contact their company again. As mentioned previously, a manufacturing company competes almost solely in terms of prices; consequently, the opportunity to compete in tenders gives manufacturers an even playing field. Once it tenders a bid, it has provided all the necessary information up front and, in this sense, it has completed its marketing duty. It is understood that the final determining factor is the price: Even a satisfied customer is not likely to return to the same manufacturing company unless the price it bid was the lowest. Manufacturing companies should provide high quality service and employ pleasant people with good communication skills, so that the client can trust them and communicate with them. However, this is not really marketing. Typical marketing via ads in the media is superfluous for manufacturing companies. Instead, they usually prefer to appeal to a number of potential customers and inform them of the type of work they do; the rest will follow.

In a product-based company, marketing is one of the main efforts. The company invests in marketing, in order to induce clients to buy its products in the nearest shop, on the internet or anywhere else. Marketing in the product-based company is focused on displaying the company's products, their advantages and values. Marketing here needs to deal with competitors and aim at differentiating the company and its products from the competitive market in which it operates.

There's no need to provide examples of how products are marketed. There have been many books written on the marketing of products and services. Instead, let us see how a manufacturing company wishing to become a product-based company should alter its marketing approach and activities.

Unfortunately, most companies consider the process of changing from manufacturing to product-focused companies to be complete once they are prepared to start marketing the product.

It is easy for the manufacturing company to decide to become a product-based company, as it is clearly understands that as a product-based company it stands to make a larger profit on the same product it already manufactures. The product will be sold in shops at a price that is thousands of percent higher than the price it quotes as a manufacturer of the product. I remember a part of an American film about a Hollywood Cinderella story, in which a girl from the slums becomes one of the richest women in America. It begins with a scene where the girl, Emma, an Afro-American, sews cloths in a small shop in the suburbs of a remote town. She finishes sewing an evening dress and hangs it on the hanger while talking to a Mexican seamstress, Sylvia, who sits next to her. Emma complains about the low wages, and that she is unable to pay the rent. Sylvia says, laughing: "If you could sell the dress at the price it will sell in the shop, you wouldn't have to work anymore this year". Emma does not understand, and Sylvia tells her that she was told by her cousin that the dresses they sew are sold to a known brand, that adds its label to the dresses and then sells them for thousands of dollars each. Emma does not believe her and the film continues. Towards the end, after Emma has become a rich business woman, she is at a prestigious cocktail party, where she speaks with a known designer, whose dress she is wearing. He tells her about the quality of the dress, the special fabrics and careful sewing invested in the dress, which raises the price to thousands of dollars. Emma's reply is the epitome of the Cinderella story: "Don't tell me your regular story, I am no regular customer. As a girl I used to sew such dresses, and I know exactly what they are worth". The seamstress who made this dress is totally unaware of its label and where it ends up, but the fact is that when the dress is complete and her job is done, the dress without the label is sold at a price that is negligible compared to the price of the labeled item.

The difficulty in changing from a manufacturing company to a product-based company does not arise at the production stage. There the production manager knows what to do to produce thousands of different products. The difficulty, which often becomes a full-fledged barrier, is in marketing. This is because the product's success depends on the very first time the client encounters both the product and the company name, since it as that point that the customer decides whether to purchase this product from company A from the competition (often both products were produced using the same machine at the same place). As we saw, manufacturing companies try to sell their products by the only marketing method they know, namely, the price. Hence, their marketing is based solely on offering the best price for the client, and not on any other aspects of marketing, such as brand building, product loyalty, making the brand a status symbol, etc.

As a result, when manufacturing companies attempt the transition to product-based companies, they often stumble at this hurdle, and can suffer a severe blow, the implications of which can affect even their manufacturing operations. The marketing strategy typical in these situations is known as "market penetration pricing"; however, it is an inappropriate strategy for companies trying to shift from a manufacturing focus to a product-based focus. This strategy is wrong for them, because it has a detrimental effect on the following:

1. The client's concept of the product
2. The product's perceived quality
3. The client's concept of the company
4. The reactions of competitors and clients.

Introducing this strategy is such a common marketing mistake, that it merits an in-depth look. In the process, we will highlight other, more useful marketing principles that should guide a company transitioning from manufacturing to product-centered marketing.

1. The client's concept of the product

Clients equate the benefits of using the product with the cost. Many studies have shown that people who have paid more for a certain product enjoyed it more than if they had paid less for it. In a famous study, students were asked to drink from two unidentified bottles of wine. One had the price tag of $100 and the other of $10. When asked which wine they enjoyed more, most of them answered that the expensive wine was tastier. They were unaware that it was the same wine in both bottles.

When potential customers find that one company sells a particular product at a much lower price than the price the competitors demand for the same product, they ask themselves: "What if this cheaper product is of a lesser quality?" Just the fact that the customer posed such a question may be enough to undermine all other marketing attempts and strategies.

2. The product's perceived quality

The second obstacle that the penetration pricing marketing strategy poses for a manufacturing company intent on shifting paradigms is its effect on the perceived quality of the product. Occasionally a product-based company may choose to lower its profit margins for a certain period, in order to introduce a product, particularly if it represents a product category or a brand that is new to the market. In such cases, the strategy can be useful, but in most of the cases I have come upon, it is a risky strategy. Not only could it kill any chance of selling the product, it could deliver a mortal blow to the company itself. Once a company launches the product at a cheap price, from that point on customers will refuse to accept it at a higher price bracket. If the company should try to raise the price on this product at a later time, the client may refuse to buy, basically because no one appreciates being made to feel like a fool. In this scenario, a potential customer would have to ask "why should I pay more for the same product that my friend bought for less?" (There is a separate case of introducing an on-off price reduction, which does not rule out raising prices later, but I won't go into it here).

To introduce a product at a lower price than that offered by the competition while maintaining as wide a profit margin as possible, the company may choose to make some "minor" alterations to the product. The objective of this type of change is to reduce the cost of production without damaging functionality. Unfortunately, such alterations may backfire, as they end up affecting the quality of the product.

This is the crux of the quality issue for a manufacturing company trying to make the shift. Typically, this company does not yet have a functional R&D department, so it does what seems like the next best thing: It takes a competing product and tries to see what it can do to manufacture it with an added attribute at a reduced cost. This process seems like a natural and easy step to the company. It has the engineers who know how to make the drawings and produce the product, or at the very least they are capable of copying the product using their own production means. The only thing they do not understand is how an R&D department works in an actual product-based company. One of the emphases of such an R&D department is the product durability. The R&D department of a product-based company will test the product to determine --and if necessary redefine-- the boundaries of its capabilities, to ascertain that it is in fact a high quality product that the customer will recommend to others even years later. The manufacturing company is unaware of these processes, and therefore may make seemingly minor changes, which may save it a lot of money, but from a broader perspective could end up killing the product.

A good friend who owns a construction company told me the following story. The company has always used only high-quality, European produced drills. One day a sales person for a tools company approached him and offered to sell him an identical drill at half the price. When he looked at the drill, it looked exactly the same, same color, same contours and even when he opened it up he saw that the motor was set to rotate in the same direction in both drills. The salesperson explained that the drill was made in the same factory in China, and if my friend wanted to save and avoid paying an extra price for the brand, it was possible to purchase it directly from China. The European brand drill was marked "made in China" and therefore there was no reason to think the drills were different. So my friend decided to purchase one as a trial. After one month, the drill stopped working in the middle of a work and my friend, who is not an engineer but with the soul and knowledge of several engineers, decided to check to see what happened. When he opened it he saw that the two cog-wheels moved, but the axle to which they were attached had broken. He told me he was surprised to find that the axle was made of metal and not of cheap plastic material, and at first glance he could not figure out what had happened. After he opened the European brand drill as well, he understood the difference between a brand-made and an unbranded product. The axle for the cog wheels in the European drill was made of a special metal alloy, which had a very low friction coefficient, high resistance to heat and the ability to stand heat and cold alternately without being affected. The unnamed brand used a simple metal axle, of the same shape but not of the same material. This "slight" change probably reduced the price of production and enabled the customer to purchase it at a lower price but in the long-term it killed the product. Even if the company were now to change the material of the axle to the original alloy, the company lost its chance for turning first time customers into clients.

3. The client's concept of the company

The concept that clients have of a company is a fundamental principle and a major consideration in the marketing efforts of both a manufacturing and a product-based company. However, in a product based company, this concept is based not only on the company's performance but also – if not more so – on the company's image. Introducing an artificially low price for the purpose of market penetration can deal a debilitating blow to the company's image. A customer who buys a cheap product from a certain company expects to find the rest of the company's products within the same price bracket. For example, Toyota produces cars for daily use, and more expensive models for managers. In addition, it produces luxury cars under the brand-name Lexus, which operates as a separate company. The lowest price for this brand is more expensive than the highest price tag for a Toyota model. The reason for operating under a separate brand name is not only to characterize a certain type of client, but also to create an affiliation between the particular type of client and the brand name. A client who comes into a sales room with both the luxury model and the family car side by side will find it difficult to pay five times more for a car with all the trimmings, when next to it there is a car with fewer trimmings, but priced on a completely different scale. However, when the luxury product is associated with its own prestigious brand, the different price scale is not a deterrent. People expect to pay a lot for the products of a certain company, and a little for the products of another. A company that enters a price niche at the lower end of the spectrum will damage its chances of future sales of higher-end products, even if they might be patent-protected products. Once a company is perceived as producing cheap products, the rest of the products will have the same reputation, and the client would not be willing to pay top prices for its products.

This is the reason that Chinese companies often opt to buy leading Western brand name companies. One of the main assets that such companies bring with them, in addition to the brand value and monetary worth, is the fact that the company has acquired a reputation for selling reliable products, so that people agree to pay high prices for products bearing that brand name. In the chapter on brands, we shall examine differences between brands of various companies, but first and foremost, a good brand is recognized by the existence of clients who are willing to purchase its products, despite a relatively high market price.

4. The reactions of competitors and clients.

After discussing the perceived association between quality and price and the manipulation of these ground rules when a company changes from a manufacturing to a product-based company, I would like to raise another issue, which is, in my opinion, the main hurdle in performing this change. Once a manufacturing company begins marketing its own products, it obviously has to compete with products already on the market. Unfortunately, some of the competing products may have been manufactured by this very same company, but marketed under a different name, that of the manufacturing company's client.

It is easy to see why a former manufacturer would be tempted to lower the price of a product introduced under the name of the newly formed product-based company. However, the mind set and the principles that guide a product-based company are of a different essence. In addition, anyone who might be aware of the company's recent transition is likely to resent the shift. Indeed, introducing a product at an artificially low price is an almost sure-fire way to call attention to the shift; it is the tell-tale act of a manufacturer.

Imagine how you'd feel if a couple of your employees decided to open their own business selling products that you taught them to make! That is the feeling that the manufacturing company's former clients experience when it is in the process of shifting into a higher paradigm: They feel betrayed. The manufacturer they have been relying on has taken their idea and is using it and knowledge of the manufacturing process to compete with them. Their immediate reaction is to sever their relations with the manufacturing company as long as it continues to produce the same products under its own name, and in addition, they often initiate a lawsuit for theft of knowledge.

At this point, the efforts of the manufacturing company usually come to an abrupt end. A manufacturing company is usually managed conservatively, since its profit margins are low. If no managerial adjustments have been made in light of the intended transition, the inevitable conclusion will be to avoid risk taking, by safeguarding the relationship with former clients and customers.

This is precisely what happened with *Ner*. The owners decided to take advantage of the company's abilities and knowledge: It took one of the products that it used to manufacture for a particular client and began to market it independently, in sectors to which the former client did not belong. However, upon visiting the company's premises, this client saw a certain advertisement about its ability to produce such a product. This client immediately announced that if *Ner* did not stop making the product for other clients, their relationship would end forthwith. *Ner* immediately stopped marketing the product to new clients. The production company does not want to lose clients, and will usually stop marketing the product and revert to a production company.

In a solutions-based company, marketing is done differently than in a product-based company. The aim of marketing here is not to sell a product, but to sell solutions which are actually the company's abilities. Marketing and selling solutions which are not tangible and clear, compared to products, is no less challenging than the marketing of either a product-based or a manufacturing company. The only advantage in this case is that the company is able to market the marginal value accrued from the use of the solutions it offers. For example, an insurance company does not market the details of the policy, but the ability to sleep soundly knowing you are safe. The solutions-based company markets the hoped for results of using its solution as if it were a product. The option of claiming ownership over the outcome of using a service is the privilege of a solutions supplier. The solutions supplier effectively appropriates one aspect of our lives, as if it were the solution being offered.

Marketing a solution is a complex mission, since it entails an overall shift that often changes the habits of both a single customer and a business client. Nevertheless, once customers assimilate the change, from that moment on their loyalty is virtually immutable. The solutions-based companies have understood this, and therefore their marketing includes extensive efforts, and their strategy hardly ever includes the reduction of prices, but rather the offering of a better solution. For example, banks try to convey the message that they can be trusted, and deal less with the commissions they charge. They understand that people rarely change from one bank to another, since people get quickly used to a good solution, and will not change unless something radical happens which makes them re-evaluate their alliance.

The message conveyed when marketing solutions is three-fold:

1. The company can be trusted.

2. The company is aware of your problem, even if you are not.

3. The company has an expert solution to your problem.

I would like to analyze two solutions to explain these messages. The first one is an advertisement I heard on the radio, for an insurance company which sells insurance for people over fifty. The second is a presentation I gave hundreds of times featuring the solutions I sold in my previous job.

Both the advertisement and the presentation begin with an explanation about the company. In the presentation I would explain about the size and strength of the company, its seniority on the market, etc. In addition, I would speak about a number of large deals that were recently closed. My aim was to impress upon the client that it was not me, Nathaniel, who was selling this solution, but Nathaniel the delegate, who represents the huge enterprise of this well-established the company. The advertisement likewise starts with the announcement "X is the largest and most professional company in this country in terms of health insurance'. These openings are intended to tell the client "here is a solution, not a product – we do not have a uniform product that fits all, but we can be trusted to find the best product suited for your needs."

Next, I would elaborate about the problem the client faced, current as well as potential future problems. In 99% of the cases, the client had never even given them a passing thought. In the insurance company advertisement the announcer asks: "do you know what happens after 50? You begin to get ill; your body does not feel so good… it can creep up on you with no warning." The advertisement aims to shake the clients out of their supposed complacency, since they might have to tackle these problems sooner than they expect, as we, the expert company, are well aware.

When clients realize and acknowledge the problem as theirs, and recognize the company as an expert authority, they are prepared to hear the third part – the solution. In my presentation, I would show the company's abilities utilized for solving problems similar to those (soon to be) encountered by the client. The parallel in the advertisement is the statement that the company can provide the necessary insurance, so that the clients can sleep well at night, at a very low cost. This is the part where the clients realize that they do not have to figure out the solution. Someone else will do it for them, in an optimal way. This is the part that binds the clients to the company.

With proper marketing, the solutions-based company name will become synonymous with professionalism and expertise in its field, so that clients who realize they have a problem, will get in touch seeking solutions.

When a product-based company wishes to market itself as a solutions company, it needs to bring true value together with the new image. Many companies present themselves as solution companies, while they are truly product-based companies. This damages their image and reliability, since clients who have been led to expect an overall solution to their problem suddenly realize they were given only a product, a tool, which may or may not bring about the desired solution, but only after they invest a lot of work to get there. These clients end up resenting both the product and the company.

Some companies do market themselves as solutions companies, but we shall discuss them later.

To summarize the marketing approach of the different company types:

- Manufacturing companies – maintain contact with the client in order to have an opportunity to compete for the next order.

- Product-based companies – address clients actively, updating them about current products and developments while emphasizing the advantages of the company's product over that of the competitors.

- Solutions-based companies – situate the company as an overall problem solver for clients, the first point of call for any problem that may arise.

MANUFACTURING, PRODUCT, SOLUTIONS

The Client

One of the main differences between companies is the type of client they target. Each company appeals to a different type of clients. This affects the company's marketing strategy, its advertising and the price range of its products or services.

As mentioned, manufacturing companies enjoy the advantage of size. Therefore they would seek clients that provide a large and constant volume of work. By contrast, a manufacturing company that deals with a large number of small clients incurs high management costs, which reduce its competitiveness.

Manufacturing companies as a rule do not have outlets, and do not sell directly to the end-customer who uses the product. This fact is noticeable in today's global economy, in which many products are transported from one country to the next, and it is impossible to know which company handled which part of the production.

The disadvantage in working with large clients is that they are usually quite knowledgeable about the manufacturing process and have high bargaining abilities. This leads them to constantly seek alternatives, and they have little loyalty to their suppliers. As a result, the manufacturing company needs to keep its prices relatively low to compete against similar manufacturers on the market.

Let me share with you some of the project management experience I gained in the company I worked for. Part of the project I managed was outsourced to a manufacturing company I shall call 'Mada', which worked with us as a sub-contractor. Mada was a model for company that supplied the products on time and at the required quality. The project progressed at a satisfactory pace. After a while, we received another large order for the same product. I met with the company director to go over the cost calculations expected for the project. When we came to Mada's share, the director informed me he believed that for an order on such a scale other suppliers on the market might quote us lower prices. He was not interested in the fact that the people at Mada were nice, or were good suppliers. He was only interested in reducing costs, even if it meant more work and a bigger headache for our company. I met with other companies, and did in fact obtain price quotes that were better than the prices we'd been paying Mada. However, since I wanted to continue to work with the company, I met with the Mada sales reps and told them of my findings. I informed them that I had cheaper offers and could not pay more. I asked them to meet the price of our best offer so that we could continue to work together. Since we were large customers, they agreed and even went a bit lower than the best price quote I had received.

This story has a happy ending in terms of the company I worked for, since it continued to get the same level of service, at a cheaper price. For Mada, this ending is not so wonderful. As a manufacturing company, its client easily found other, cheaper alternatives. Given that it has no technological or other advantage in the market, it is in an inferior position, and therefore it was forced to agree to do the same work for less.

This story exemplifies the problematic of being a manufacturing company. Manufacturing companies are always completely at the mercy of their clients, and have no real leverage to help them make larger profits.

The story is quite different for product-based companies. In these companies we finally meet the end client, who in this case is the target of all their efforts. Product-based companies' level of sophistication requires that they employ agents and distribution systems, which hardly ever exist in manufacturing firms.

The product-based company makes products, sees that they are placed on shelves and waits for the customers to come and purchase the products. In this sense, the company is passive, but even more so, the customers are passive. They are not initiators; they expect the company's products to be readily available at an agreed on location. A company that produces sugar does not expect customers to come to the plant to buy the product; it sees to it that the product is brought to the supermarket and placed on the appropriate shelves.

To reach the passive customers requires a wide network through which to distribute the products, so as to reach as many potential clients as possible. This distribution may be done by the product company itself or through a sub-contractor (a manufacturing company in its own right), which provides distribution services to the different outlets. The manufacturing advantage of the distributor is usually that of size: Since it works with large number products, the marginal cost of distribution for each product is lower. Once the products reach their end station in the shop, they should be stored on the shelves and the sales environment must be maintained as well. These tasks also cost money. At the end of the day, the distribution process usually means that a product-based company needs at least two mediators between itself and the end customer.

There is hardly any direct contact between the product-based company and the end customer, which is why distributors and shop owners are often referred to as the company's true clients. If a company decides to raise the price of its product, the first to complain will be the shop owners, since it is likely that they will sell less of the said product. The product-based company needs to consider the shop owners, even if the latter do not purchase the products for cash, but by consignation. If a shop owner's expectations are not met by a certain supplier, the shop owner will not place that supplier's products on the shelves at priority locations (if at all), and will thus lead customers to choose the competition's products, products which afford the store owner a wider profit margin. A perfect example is the case of travel agents and tourism companies, which will work hard to convince you to purchase a holiday in a specific hotel or fly with a certain airline. Even though there might be better deals out there for you, the company pushes the deals that bring in a better profit.

As noted, product-based companies need to play a double game and cater to two different types of clients, although there is only a single compensation. The companies' front-line customer is the shop owner. This customer must be convinced that this specific product will give the best benefits, surpassing all other products in the same category, and therefore it is a worthwhile investment. The shop's investment in the product is the shelf space, location and internal advertising in the shop. A product-based company that fails to convince the shop owner to introduce this product into the shop and to place it in a strategic location cannot reach the next customer down the line.

In order to induce the first customer, the shop owner, to "pay for" or invest resources in the product, companies need to invest in sales tactics no less than they invest in the end customer. For example, a company that produced toiletries wanted to penetrate the market. It ran an ad with two main messages: "you can find our products only in the best shops", and "don't forget to look for our products at a store near you". The main purpose was to get shop owners to understand, that if they are asked by the company to introduce this product in their shops, they will be identified as a good shop and that makes it worth their while to place the product there. In addition, the ad was intended to create pressure on the shop owners from the bottom up, through the customers' demand. Even well-known phrases such as "the best selling product in America" or "the world's leading brand" are meant to target the shop owners as well as the end customers. When the shop owners do not believe that a product is capable of reaching a high sales volume, a product-based company will try to lure them in by offering a relatively wide profit margin, thus reducing its own profits in the process. This leads to a vicious circle: the more well-known a product is and the greater the customer demand, the more pressure can be placed on the retailer to reduce the profit margin. This is the case of an anchor product: Without it, the retailer will find it nearly impossible to reel in any customers, as they will choose to shop where this product can be found. For example, retailers make a very small profit on anchor products such as bread and milk, but if they didn't sell these products, customers simply wouldn't shop there at all.

Thus, product-based companies' particular relationship with their dual customers requires them to build whole advertising and image campaigns around the product, so that it virtually sells itself and is distinct from the competing product. The passive client's decision to buy one product and not the others on the shelf is made instinctively and does not involve too many rational processes.

In contrast, solutions-based companies' clients are active. Active clients involve themselves in the purchasing process on many levels, from arriving and waiting in line for a service, to running tests and experiments to examine the solution.

Solutions-based companies can have different types of clients: they might sell only to institutional clients, governmental clients or private clients, but the companies' approach is the same. It is not possible to sell a solution by describing it; instead the primarily focus of the sale must be on the problem and the result after the solution has been implemented. Active clients want to know *what* they're paying for (rather than how much it cost to produce the solution), and that *what* is the end result.

Let us take for example the company called Aeronautics. It grew from being a small manufacturing company that sold small unmanned aerial vehicles (UAVs) to a large solutions-based company that sells UAV photos. When it was only a UAV manufacturer, the company applied to the IDF, its major client, with an offer to privatize the UAV service. The offer was based on the fact that for the IDF to maintain a UAV squadron, it had to cover additional expenses, including manpower, overhead, service and maintenance. Instead, with Aeronautics, the IDF could purchase the end product – the photos themselves-- directly. The scope of the savings gained by sidestepping the cost of operating the UAV squadrons was significant indeed, and the solution the IDF received was a comprehensive one, which corresponded to its precise needs: The IDF could now obtain high quality aerial photographs without any primary investment or maintenance costs. Aeronautics shifted from being a product manufacturer to a solutions supplier, and the percentage of its gross profit rose sharply. The advantage of being the first to come up with this solution gave Aeronautics a span of several years until the competitors began offering the IDF the same service, and in that interim period, Aeronautics made a great deal of money.

It takes a lot of effort to motivate clients to take action; therefore, the investment in every single client is substantial. However, since the companies that are called upon to make such an investment are solutions-based companies, the expected profit is also significant.

To summarize, each type of company targets a different type of client:

- Manufacturing companies – are at the mercy of a few knowledgeable clients.

- Product-based companies – have passive clients who congregate at an external location.

- Solutions-based companies –invest in active clients who are interested in the quality of the solution.

Advertising

After observing the differences between types of companies and the marketing messages they wish to convey to the various types of clients, let us examine the differences in the type of advertising used and the placement of the ads.

Manufacturing companies advertise only to large clients, since they bring in the most revenue. These clients expect to receive information on manufacturing companies mostly in a professional environment, and therefore it is rare to see such advertisements on the streets, but only in professional magazines and on relevant Internet sites.

A manufacturing company's advertisements emphasize its capabilities and the list of its current customers. The latter serves as proof of the company's ability to produce at a high level. The prime concern of a firm that orders a product from a manufacturing company is that the quality of the product might not meet its standards. Therefore, a manufacturer that can boast of having well known customers with an established reputation gives potential clients the assurance that they are in a good company.

The objective of advertising in general is to make the standard customer feel that "everybody is already there, except me". It doesn't matter whether the advertisement is for a manufacturing, product-based or solutions-based company. The effect advertisers use with the highest frequency is the herd effect. We all want to run together, dress the same way, look the same, and if possible, to be most of the same, in other words, stand out – within the herd. This effect is used in horse and dog races. The reason why the horse naturally tries to lead the herd is that its instinctive behavior is to avoid predators and run as quickly as possible, since the one that is last is the one that will get caught. We all want to be first; therefore, companies will tell us that it is cool to move production to India, wear certain items, undergo surgery or remove chest hair. In each case, whether advertising a manufacturer, a product or a solution, the advertising message addresses our wish to be like everybody else, and if we can be the ones to most resemble everyone else --better yet!

Of the three company types, product-based companies engage in the most widespread advertising, since they wish to reach all potential clients, introduce insights and behaviors into our subconscious, so that we will choose their product over that of the competitors. Product-based companies' advertisements always present the advantages of the product, or demonstrate its quality. The demonstration can be direct, by showing how a detergent can remove all stains, or by comparison, where the advertisement shows how the famous detergent is far better than the competition. When advertising a product, the "*proof* of the *pudding* is in the eating", or even in the indirect outcome of "eating". Thus, the message might be: "if you use our instant pudding, the entire family will be grateful, yet the product's advantages are also emphasized (tasty, easy to make). Furthermore, product-based companies' advertisements also try to introduce certain behaviors through our subconscious. Consequently, almost every advertisement shows a customer (always a good looking model who represents us--the consumers) taking the product off the supermarket shelf with a smile and placing it in the shopping cart. The aim is to make us repeat this action and put the product in the cart the next time we visit the supermarket, all the while hoping that we too look like the model…

The second component of the advertisement is the reinforcement of the brand name. In manufacturing companies' advertisements, the brand name is hardly ever emphasized, since it is much less important than it is in product-based companies, in which case it becomes almost critical. The product-based companies try to convey through the brand name much of what the product represents, and thus, the client's familiarity with the name is manipulated for the sake of increasing sales. A company that produced chocolate milk over the years and now wishes to produce other dairy treats will emphasize the pleasure derived from drinking chocolate milk and will use the same description to characterize the eating of the dairy treats. In this manner, the description serves as an anchor, through which the new product can be introduced into the market. The brand name should be mentioned often: This helps make the product that is the subject of the advertisement seem familiar, and increases its perceived value in the eyes of the customers.

In solutions-based companies, advertising does not seek to explain fully what the customer receives. The solutions-based company wants to emphasize its professional standards and the problems it can solve for the client (problems of which the customer is often unaware). Finally, the client is shown the end result.

My favorite advertisement on the Israeli television this week is the one with the Bank Mizrahi client called Dvir. Dvir sits on a swing in his garden and tells his wife there is one thing he does not discuss with his best friend, but does so with the true professionals of the Mizrahi-Tefahot Bank. He tells her that when he chooses a lifelong mortgage, he trusts them to do their very best, and as a result, he is able to pay the least possible. This establishes the bank's professional capabilities and the result. Then he takes out two airline tickets and tells her that with the money the bank helped them save, they can take can afford a vacation in Manchester --the effect of the result. Finally he delivers the punch line: He takes out the Manchester United scarf and tells her he already has the tickets to the Champions League game, about which she appears much less enthusiastic...

Another example is the advertisement for hair removal. We do not see the tool by which the hair is removed or any pictures of the process, but only the result, and the company's promise that the customer will continue to enjoy the result for some time after the treatment is completed.

The objective of the solutions-based company in advertising is primarily to reinforce the message that the brand means professionalism, and the fact that the company can be relied on. The most important impression that the company wants to create is that it alone knows exactly what the client needs and that it is the best choice for the job. Therefore, the advertisements of a solutions-based company, such as a bank, will emphasize that in certain situations one shouldn't trust close friends, but can safely rely on the service of true professionals, in this case, the bank.

The next stage of the process is to explain the problem to the client. As we all know, identifying the problem is already 50% of the solution. The solutions-based company wants to be associated with the solution already at the problem stage, but it manipulates this association to suit its own purposes. Thus, returning to the example of the bank commercial described earlier, it is clear to all that shortage of money is a general problem shared by many, but the bank channels the problem to the subject of mortgages, and life-long mortgages, at that. The client then thinks: "if they have identified the problem, they probably have the solution".

In the third stage, the solutions company presents the result, the solution of the problem. It does not mention how much the solution costs, nor does it mention the competition. The solution company presents itself as an island of stability, which can be trusted to lead to the desired results. Of course the result, the vacation, is one that appeals to everyone. Only the final punch is directed at men, who surveys tell us are the ones that make most of the family's financial decisions.

To summarize, in

- Manufacturing companies – advertising is limited to specific clients and focuses on the company's capabilities.

- Product-based companies – advertising takes a broader perspective and shows the product's advantages and abilities in view of the competition, while reinforcing the brand name.

- Solutions-based companies – uses the widest scope of advertising, to emphasize brand reinforcement, establish the company's professional experience and demonstrate the end-result.

As an addendum, I would like to remind you that there many imitations and counterfeits in the world. I do not mean just copying products of famous brands, but copying a company's specific positioning within the market.

Often, a product advertisement made by a product-based company presents the product as a solution, in an attempt to present itself as a solutions-based company. The implications derived from this misrepresentation directly benefit the company. As shown, a solutions-based company can enjoy higher profit margins, as well as customer loyalty. Certain product-based companies are incapable of creating solutions in their current circumstances, and instead of taking the necessary steps to become solution-based, they try to offer the same product or service under the guise of a solutions provider. I shall mention one salient example, although there are many.

Coca-Cola is a classic product company by any criterion. It sells a simple product and sells it through its distributors to passive clients in many outlets. For the customers, the result will be the same whether they choose to drink Coke, Pepsi or just sweetened water – they will no longer be thirsty, and presumably take in a lot of extra calories. However, since the company wants customers to pay more for its products and aims to steer customers away from competing imitations, it tries to convince customers that it actually provides a solution (usually without defining the problem). The company's advertisements do not present a person who is thirsty, then drinks, and as a result is no longer thirsty. This would be the solution the customer requires, with no advantage to the Coca-Cola Company. Instead, the company's advertisements shift their focus in a way that makes customers forget this basic aim of thirst quenching and leads them to think of Coca-Cola's beverages as a solution to all problems. Thus, for example, some of the company's past slogans included "Things Go Better with Coke" (1963) and "Coke Adds Life" (1976). The company does not try to demonstrate what "goes better" or to provide a scientific explanation of how it "adds" or prolongs life. Instead, it shows many people doing the kind of things we would all like to do –dancing, smiling, having fun. The company uses only the final part of the solutions-based ad: It shows how we'd look after the solution, but refrains from presenting the problem alongside the solution. Currently the Coca-Cola slogan is "Open Happiness", which is as unrelated as ever to the actual result of having a soft drink. This attempt to position itself --and be perceived-- as a solutions-based company becomes clear; the purpose is to bolster the brand, which is, after all, the highest valued brand in the world.

In sum, we should distinguish between impostors and companies that are truly solutions providers. This masquerading can include product-based companies posing as solutions providers and manufacturers posing as product-based companies. Eventually the pretense is exposed and the company loses credit with the customers. There are however cases in which the pretense of product-based companies posing as solutions-based companies does not end up deterring customers. This is because the customers are very much aware of the hype and they know all along that they are being sold something that does not really exist. Consequently, they are not disappointed when after downing a can of Coke they still need to quench their thirst with a glass of tap water.

The Brand

Manufacturing companies pay less attention to the brand under which the company produces. It is accustomed to manufacturing for other brand names, and that's why its own brand is left unattended. The brand is neglected because branding is important when targeting private customers, and less so for companies that target other firms, specifically, product-based companies. Almost all of the manufacturing companies in the world emphasize the same benefits: "Quality, speed, and price". A manufacturing company that wishes to brand itself usually uses the company's name. Typically, manufacturing companies operate according to the ancient Jewish rule that states "A good name is better than riches", in other words, a reputation is one's most important asset, and in this case, it's even more important than the merchandise one provides. Basically, if someone has a good reputation the chances are that this person provides the merchandise to match, and therefore customers are willing to pay for that merchandise. Manufacturing companies do not emphasize the brand name in their advertising, since they count on recognition of the company name as sufficient collateral to make a potential customer contact the company.

A good brand is supported by clients and co-workers, as in the proverb "let another praise you and not your own mouth;" therefore, manufacturing companies go to lengths to highlight the list of their clients. This list is testimony to the strength of the brand: the longer the list, the higher the chances that a potential client will call.

Let's go back to our manufacturing company, Ner. We see that it cannot add its name on the products it makes, because clients object. Given that the clients are product-based companies, the presence of another, additional brand name on the product they sell is apt to cause them damage. Manufacturing companies are therefore not allowed to present their own brand name to the public, and in effect, this absence might cause them to lose potential clients. Under these circumstances, they prefer to invest their efforts to attract new clients be means other than strengthening the brand name.

The brand is an important component in a product-based company's ability to sell and be selected over the competition. Returning to the Coca-Cola example, we see that the value of the Coca-Cola brand is almost equal to the company's market value. What can be inferred from this fact is no less than amazing: Customers care less about what they're drinking as long as it features the brand name Coca-Cola. A brand name is stronger than the product or any of its manufacturing sites. Investors estimate that a company without a brand name is almost worthless and, inversely, if the company were to sell the use of its brand name, the brand would continue to bring in profits approximately at the same rate as its current earnings. This is an extreme example of the significance of the brand name. The brand name --along with its implied meanings-- is what makes us choose a certain beverage in the vendor's refrigerator over all the other options there. The reason people reach the purchasing stage is identical – to fulfill a certain need, thirst in our case. No one buys Coca-Cola for any other reason. However, the outcome of the purchasing stage, in which a choice must be made and one product is selected over other options, this outcome is based entirely on the brand.

The brand and support of the brand are crucial for persuading passive clients. The brand gives customers the illusion that this particular product can deliver a solution that addresses their basic need better than any other product can.

A branded product costs more than other products for two reasons. The actual reason is that usually only companies that produce a high quality product bother to invest in branding. Customers are not fools: If the product does not correspond to their basic need the first time they purchase it, they will not make the same mistake twice. For example, if a car company is perfectly branded, but the actual driving does not fulfill the customer's expectations, the company's investment in the branding will be for naught, because rumors of a bad purchase spread quickly in the world we live in. Therefore, only brands which have the goods can actually afford to invest in branding. The other reason that branded products are more expensive is that having invested significantly in marketing their brand, companies now have to compensate for the expense in some way, and absorbing it in the price ticket –that is, reaching into the client's pocket-- is the perfect way to do so. And that's the way the cookie crumbles.

The crucial point mentioned in passing in the above paragraph regarding brands is the relationship between expectation and result. A brand creates for us a certain expectation. We expect a Cartier watch to look prestigious and work perfectly. An un-branded watch that stops working after a year will elicit an extremely different reaction from that evoked if a Cartier watch stopped working. A client expects to get a certain value with the brand; therefore, a brand that does not fulfill these expectations will suffer. When branding themselves, product-based companies must be sure they can create the experience they promise the customer. Product-based companies should work from the bottom up, so that performance and brand values correlate naturally, rather than raise expectations which cannot be fulfilled and then crash the brand entirely.

A unique and important characteristic of product-based companies is the ability to disconnect the brand-name from the company's name. Some product-based companies have several brands, each addressing a different market segment and expressing other brand values. Car manufacturers are champions in creating this separation, in that almost every car company has a main brand and a luxury brand. Some popular examples are Toyota and Lexus; Nissan and Infinity; GM which has the Buick and the Cadillac; Ford and Lincoln; and the Volkswagen, Bugatti, and Porsche. Manufacturing and solutions-based companies cannot separate the company name from the brand name, since the most distinguishing feature of the former is the company's name and abilities, whereas that of the latter is its knowledge and reliability. Therefore, there is no point for either manufacturers or solutions-based companies to create a brand that is disassociated from the company. Therefore, only product-based companies can benefit from separating the company name from the brand name.

The branding in a solutions-based company is again different matter. There it is no less important than in product-based companies, but the uses and the attitudes are different. Some solutions-based companies do not invest at all in publicizing their brand, since they solve clients' problems, often in a unique way, and thus the positive reinforcement for their brand comes directly from the clients.

An example of solutions-based industries or individuals that have a strong brand but do not need to advertise are those which offer solutions of a spiritual nature. Rabbis, a priests, cadis and shamans offer solutions to many people's problems without advertising themselves, and while the value of their brand is not quite clear, people nevertheless approach them in the hope of obtaining a complete solution to their problems and woes. The advantage of these spiritual solutions providers is that even a small portion of success, which usually cannot even be proven, builds their brand so strongly that people tend to seek their services and promote their brand disproportionately.

The branding of solutions-based companies doesn't rely on evoking a range of images, since they do provide an actual solution and not just an illusion. For example, private physician and hospitals do not need to promote health as part of their brand value, since by definition, this is what they do – promote health. In contrast, manufacturers of herbal based medicines which lack scientific proof to back them up or healers with no proof of healing will use the values of health, medicine, and wellbeing in creating their brand, in an attempt to bolster their image and allow them to compete with the level of professionalism offered by representatives of conventional, institutionalized medicine.

The brand in a solutions-based company needs to describe the benefit to the customer, and therefore the images and emotions used to promote the brand are related directly – rather than implicitly, as in product-based companies – to the solution afforded by the product. Rather, the purpose is to convey the company's professionalism and its ability to solve the clients' problems. The clients imagine (independently, or aided by the brand's symbol, slogan, etc.) how they will feel when the problem is solved. What induces the customer to buy the solution is the prospect of the image or feeling that comes with the end result. This manner of advertising is distinct from that used by product-based companies, where the experiences projected to the client by the brand are palpably distant from the actual outcome or value. Just today I watched a TV commercial for a particular car. It showed a guy in a Peugeot who at the stop-light meets a girl who's also driving a Peugeot. Their interaction conveys the sexual interest and tension between them. This advertisement communicates the message that Peugeot is a car for young people, and it will make you attractive to members of the opposite sex. In the real world, it is obvious to viewers and potential customers that driving a Peugeot does not guarantee an encounter --fortuitous or otherwise-- with an attractive model. Nonetheless, the product-based company intentionally creates a sensation that is not directly related to the actual product or to its significance for the customer. Conversely, in a solutions-based company such as communication providers, the solution offered is described precisely, such as the ability to connect with family members. The fact that customers agree to pay more for a good solution obviates the need to make them pay more for an experience that will never happen.

To summarize, in

- Manufacturing companies – the brand name is usually the name of the company, and the message conveyed is the quality of the work and the price.

- Product-based companies – the role of the brand is to indicate a new product, which is on the same level as the rest of the products under that brand name.

- Solutions-based companies – the brand is completely identified with the company, conveying a message of expertise and professionalism in a particular area.

Intellectual Property

The changes in the world over the past two centuries have changed the map of assets and wealth unrecognizably.

Until 250 years ago, compensation for work was usually related to the employee's ability to exert physical strength – this was the state of affairs for centuries, from the Roman slave markets to the industrial revolution. The stronger the employee, the taller and bigger he was, the higher his output. In the industrial revolution, machine owners became capitalists, and physical strength was replaced by intellectual abilities. In a similar pattern, until about a hundred years ago, the value of land was mainly determined by its size and quality and less by its location. Land was a manufacturing resource; therefore, the more lands you had, and the more productive they were, the greater their worth. Since then, the world has changed and, currently, a square meter in Manhattan or Hong Kong on the thirtieth floor of a high-rise, where nothing can grow, is worth as much as thousands of square meters of fertile agricultural land in Brazil.

In today's world, the value of a brand, which is no more than a design on a logo, can be worth more than tons of gold.

Nowadays, the name of Albert Einstein is at the tip of everyone's tongue, but few know the name of the person that won that last Iron man competition. Today Stephen Hawking, a scientist who is unable to move a single limb in his body, but whose brain works admirably, is more respected than the best boxer in the world.

We live in the age of knowledge.

Today our concepts about the value of assets change rapidly. Global expenditure on medication is higher than 8311 tons of gold, the amount of gold held by the US treasury. The value of *Facebook*, which is merely an Internet site with a yearly profit of three billion dollars is valued at a total of one hundred billion dollars.

Currently, companies understand that their main asset is the knowledge they accumulate. The knowledge can vary radically from one company to another, but a company without knowledge is a company without a future.

Today's greatest advantage is that the amount of knowledge grows exponentially, but so does our ability to access it. Before the Internet, I could not have written this book. Before the Internet age, only those who had decades of life experience could write books, not necessarily because they were smarter than members of the younger generation, but because they had accumulated more knowledge. Such knowledge is the basis for writing any book that strives to analyze situations and examples. You cannot base a book on only one or two examples; however, in a world where you can find numerous examples for any topic in the world, the leverage of years of accumulated experience decreases. The knowledge accumulated on the Internet is endless, and it is no wonder then that Google and other companies earn as much as they do just from organizing it and making it accessible. Imagine for a moment, what would all the knowledge accumulated in your brain be worth if you could not retrieve it?

Undoubtedly, knowledge is an asset, and since it cannot be perceived with the senses --not to mention – quantified, it is defined as intellectual property.

Intellectual property in a manufacturing company is very basic. The company knows how to do what the customer requires and there are thousands of other companies like it that can do precisely the same thing. This means that the intellectual property that the client possesses is of higher value than that of the manufacturer. As discussed in the chapter on knowledge, the knowledge that the manufacturing company has is limited to the functions it performs; it knows virtually nothing about the object on which it performs these functions.

In any company, the employees are those who possess the necessary knowledge. The entire scope of a company's knowledge itself can easily be documented, but only people have the capacity to integrate this knowledge and put it to use. No computer in the world that can replace a human being in terms of associative knowledge and intuition based on accumulated experience.

If a company's employees can easily be replaced, and the entire company can be transferred from one country to another with virtually no risk involved, the level and scope of knowledge in this company is apparently limited, and we are probably dealing with a manufacturing company. The threshold of knowledge required to open a new manufacturing company is low, and therefore the contribution of this knowledge to the value of the company is not significant.

In product-based companies, the value and composition of the intellectual property vary from one firm to another. In these companies, the intellectual property constitutes a significant percentage of the company's worth. Intellectual property in a product-based company is manifested in one of two pays, either in the form of a patent or as know-how, that is, the company possesses knowledge of how to do something, and although not patented, it is difficult for others to either do the same thing or even imitate it. Each category, patented knowledge and know-how, has two parts: knowledge about the manufacturing of the product, and knowledge about its use. In addition, the value of the company brand and its commercial insignia may be major contributors to the company's worth.

Registering a patent is the most common way to protect the firm's knowledge. A patent is a process whereby the company can safeguard the knowledge it has accumulated, for a period of 20 years, and give itself a significant market advantage. Sometimes the quality of a company's patents is a more significant determinant of its value than is its sales volume. An example may be seen in a pharmaceutical company that patents a certain drug. The value of its shares rises sharply, because at that point in time it has a unique product on the market. Product-based companies can have patents relating to the way the product is used, as for example in the "double-click" on the computer mouse, or relating to the manufacturing process, such as injection molding of plastic parts. Each of these patents gives the company a great advantage and the value of the patents is a crucial component in the company's net worth.

Preserving intellectual property in the form of know-how is somewhat risky, but at the same time it is more rewarding financially. Our friendly product, Coca-Cola, provides the most famous example of a superb strategy for protecting know-how. Coca-Cola's decision not to register a patent of the formula by which it produces the concentrate for its beverage turned out to be a huge success. Currently, very few people in the world know the recipe for manufacturing Coca-Cola, and this secret is the basis of the company's sales. Had the company registered a patent a hundred years ago, the knowledge would have been released into the public domain already eighty years ago, and anyone could have copied the recipe and sold it without any restriction. Therefore, the decision not to register the patent proved very successful. But the risk of this method is also huge – if the knowledge is discovered by retrospective engineering, it may be used immediately, without even a waiting period. Product-based companies occasionally opt for this method, but the considerations to do so should be carefully weighed before launching a product protected only by know-how and not by a patent.

The product-based company that wishes to survive must continuously produce new knowledge. This is done by the R&D departments and constantly fuelled by the marketing department, which feels the pulse of the customers. Earlier, we discussed the issue of transferring a company from one location to another. This is possible in a product-based company as well, but without the R&D and marketing divisions. I remember a sentence I read in Lee Iacocca's book about his success in rescuing Chrysler's from bankruptcy: he stated that all he needed to establish a new company that would achieve the same growth as Chrysler was a marketing department. At the end of the day, product-based companies' most important asset lies with the R&D and marketing departments, without which the company is merely a manufacturer.

In product-based and solutions-based companies, the brand name and the commercial insignia constitute an additional aspect of intellectual property. As mentioned in the section on branding, some companies' main value stems from their brand name; hence, a brand must be considered intellectual property.

Everyone knows the value of a commercial trademark. A garment with the label of a known designer costs several times more than the same garment would without the logo. How much do you think Apple's bitten apple is worth, or the five rings of the Olympic Games' symbol? I learned this lesson in the forgers' market of a certain Asian country I visited as part of my job. As my stay drew to a close, I went to buy gifts for my siblings in Israel. I selected two identical travel packs, only to discover that the price of one was double that of the other. When I asked the merchant about this, he replied: "can't you see that this one is by Lowe Alpine?" Of course it wasn't actually a product of Lowe Alpine, but someone had sewn on one a fake Lowe logo. It might have been news to me at that time, but there was nothing new about the power of a trademark. A neighbor told me that thirty years ago he had funded his entire trip to the East (before the forgery phenomenon spread there) with a small pouch filled with little Lacoste crocodiles, which he had received from a friend who used to work for the original company. Wherever he went, he'd buy some locally made cheap polo shirts and sew on the crocodile logo. With the refurbished shirts he bartered for accommodations, meals and anything else he needed, and although the locals knew the shirts were fake imitations, they still considered them valuable.

The value of knowledge in a solutions-based company is enormous. Often such a company cannot produce anything but knowledge, which is its only source of revenue. In solutions-based companies, knowledge includes more than the brand and logo as mentioned previously, or knowledge regarding the production and use of a product. Knowledge in the context of these companies is much more complex and sophisticated. The knowledge accumulated in this case concerns customers' general behavior in relation to the product, and the next problems they are bound to encounter. Customers expect the solutions-based company to solve integrative rather than discrete problems; therefore the knowledge accumulated is integrative as well. Returning to the chapter on documentation, we noted that a solutions-based company documents almost every detail, in order to provide its customers with solutions to problems they have not yet considered, or even thought of. In a solutions-based company, knowledge requires understanding the emerging trends, rather than just sporadic events.

The company thus possesses an enormous amount of information, which it converts to practical knowledge, in order to seek the solutions. The information accumulated is one of the company's main assets.

It may seem, however, that the threshold of knowledge required in order to become a solutions-based company is not overwhelmingly high. Such companies do not produce anything except advice or the integration of a number of products made by others. Therefore, it is tempting to assume "if they can do it I can do it", and that success will be waiting around the next corner. This, however, would be a very grave mistake. As noted, in the solutions-based company, the accumulated knowledge and experience are the most important asset. Therefore an employee who opts to open a company independently will soon discover that there is no substitution for the experience and information required to solve the problems. Take Facebook, for example: ostensibly, all it does is provide a simple means of connecting between friends, but an in-depth examination reveals that dozens of companies have tried to do to achieve this before, whether through instant messages, chats or blogs. The ability to provide the best and most comprehensive solution requires analyzing the information correctly and building the definitive solution, which (with a little bit of luck) can cause users to become addicted. Facebook could not have been established in the early days of the Internet, since there was not yet a critical mass of users to maintain such a site. In addition, the developers and the surfers needed time to figure out the optimal way to establish contact and update the entire community about your "status". Google Wave is an example of a solution that failed to fully understand the Internet users, although it was developed by people who had already identified Internet trends. What was missing was enough accumulated knowledge about how people wanted to mail each other and the type of service they were willing to join. Indeed, even the Internet generation can be conservative about some things!

To summarize, the locus and nature of knowledge is different in each type of company.

- Manufacturing companies – possess unsophisticated knowledge, and the more valuable intellectual property is owned by the client.

- Product-based companies – the knowledge relates to a specific product, but the intellectual property is owned by the company itself.

- Solutions-based companies – accumulate enough knowledge to identify comprehensive trends that relate not only to the product but also to the clients' general environment; hence, the intellectual property is the company's major source of value.

The Company Structure

I have told you about Fib and its decision to make changes in an attempt to shift from being a manufacturing company to a product-based and solutions-based company. My first role there was as a field demonstrator of company products, positioned directly under the CEO and the company owners. At the time, the company employed eighty people in various departments. The department heads were not managers in the classical sense; rather, their position could be described as "first among equals," in other words, they were assembly line workers who had more responsibility than did the other employees, due to their level of expertise. The actual managerial responsibilities were handled by the CEO.

When I left, five years later, the company structure included three vice-presidents □ for marketing, development, and operations, who were fully responsible for the work of their subordinates.

The process of structural change did not take place overnight, and most of it was not planned. At some point, the CEO had discovered that as the number of people in the R&D department had grown, and that he could no longer manage them. The same was true for the marketing department, which demanded plenty of expensive management time. Therefore, he appointed a vice-president in charge of marketing. The process Fib underwent was to changing from a manufacturing to a product-based company. In manufacturing companies, most employees are assembly line workers and petty managers. The CEO's ability to control such a firm personally is relatively high, as long as there are professional people in the field, and he only has to deal with management issues. In such a company, there is almost no difficult-to-replace R&D or marketing staff, and therefore there is no need for managers to oversee the functioning of these departments. As mentioned in a previous section, in manufacturing companies, almost any employee can be replaced within a short period of time; therefore, since the employees' level of knowledge is not essential to the company, and thus management problems are mostly among the professional ranks.

In addition, the profit margin of manufacturing companies is not broad enough to hire managers, whose job would be to make the CEO's life easier. The recruitment of any superfluous employees and mainly of highly paid managers would have a direct effect on the company's profits, and therefore such decisions are not made lightly.

In product-based companies, R&D and marketing departments play a significant role, in terms of both importance and cost. The management of skilled and demanding people requires a lot of time, beyond what the CEO can afford to handle alone. In a product-based company, since the of the R&D and marketing personnel have an important function, the managers of these departments must invest a significant portion of their time ensuring employee satisfaction and finding new challenges and promotion schemes to keep them in the company. In addition, internal competition is an inherent characteristic of these two departments, and a manager with experience in a manufacturing company will encounter new challenges managing these departments in a product-based company. The role of managers in product-based companies is to retain the better employees and maximize their output and creativity. In recruiting personnel for a product-based company, managers pay a great deal of attention to candidates' ability to work in a team, in order to reduce the need to handle interpersonal issues later.

In a solutions-based company, the marketing and R&D functions are more important than that of production, and therefore when the company undergoes a paradigm shift, the status of the vice-presidents of these departments increases, as does the number of employees under their supervision. This is true not only in hi-tech companies, where the percentage of R&D people may reach 90%, but also in other types of solutions-based companies, where the production part is smaller in relation to the rest of the company.

Reorganization is a common concept, mainly when a new CEO comes to aid a faltering organization. I have not come upon any case in which the term has been used to describe the recruitment of new personnel; rather, is known as a code word for mass dismissals. In manufacturing companies, there is almost no need for *reorganization*, since efficient allocation of employees for production is straight forward and uncomplicated, such that a company's operations are easily maintained at an optimal level. The company's manufacturing ability is directly affected by any employee who leaves. Thus, in the context of manufacturing companies, *reorganization* may mean the purchase of new machines to replace workers, dismissals in case of decreased work load, or the recruitment of new employees to extend production. This is usually not defined as *reorganization* but as extension.

Reorganization is becoming a more frequent phenomenon in struggling product-based companies, and is seen especially in the R&D and marketing departments. Its implementation is even more noticeable in solutions-based companies. In product- and solutions-based companies, the short term profit margins may be extended at the expense of the future profits; thus, this option is attractive to managers of struggling businesses, who fear the results reported in the coming quarter. Reorganization provides a way to suddenly demonstrate higher profit margins. In solutions-based companies, it is relatively easy to dismiss those who are considered part of the company's layer of extra padding. The company can remain confident that its customers will continue to pay for its products, even if there are fewer employees available to examine how the product is used in the home or what new problems customers may be facing. The reduction in labor costs in the departments of R&D and marketing is immediately apparent in the profit and loss reports. With every employee that is dismissed, company's profits increase, which is why *Reorganization* has become such a frequently heard and familiar term.

The gravest error in the reorganization of product- and solutions-based companies is the absence of a long-term vision. Without this, the company is liable to damage its own ability to remain at the forefront of innovation, which in turn could enable competitors to increase their market share by providing better or more advanced solutions. Reorganization in its commonly used meaning should be the last step taken in an attempt to save a company and not as a means to secure short-term profits. Remember: A company that damages its R&D and marketing infrastructure sacrifices its long term vision for a quick fix .

To summarize –

- A manufacturing company consists mainly of production and operations; the departments of management, marketing and finance constitute a much smaller portion of the company and are directly subordinate to the CEO.

- A product-based company has a need for two relatively small departments --for marketing and R&D, which are hierarchically above the manufacturing level.

- A solutions-based company must have stronger marketing and R&D departments, which play a more significant role than does the manufacturing branch or department.

Quality Control

Quality control is important for any customer, and some clients may choose which company to work with based on quality control level. It is no coincidence that large customers, such as government offices and armies, require that their suppliers' quality control departments be able to adhere to the ISO 9001 quality standard.

Quality control, even under the ISO 9001 standard, differs substantially between manufacturing, product-based and solutions-based companies, in terms of test duration, the amount of resources allocated to and the people who conduct the control.

Returning again to our example of the company Ner, the tailor or seamstress seated at the sewing machine needs to verify that the stitches that were sewn indeed coincide with the required dimensions specified in the customer-provided drawing. In other words, the control is conducted by the person who has done the work, as soon as the work is completed. Quality control in these cases does not necessarily include the quality of the stitch or its type, since the instructions in the drawing include only the dimensions. In other words, the person performing the job does not have sufficient information to conduct a full-scale quality control test. Furthermore, when the quality control is done by the same person who did the job, there is a conflict of interest, since this person will have a vested interest in claiming that the job was done properly; it is much like asking the cat to guard the cream.

In a manufacturing company, quality control is done by comparing the finished product against the drawing received from the client. If the product and the drawing are the same, the company has fulfilled its mission. This is also the reason why a manufacturing company will not start producing until it gets the drawings from the client – the client can always sue if the product does not correspond to the specified needs. The quality examination in a manufacturing company is performed immediately after production by employees with basic skills and is short process. The manufacturing company is not responsible towards the end user; therefore its level of attention to the QA issue is relatively small.

In the product-based company, the responsibility is towards the end customer; therefore the company cannot claim to "work to spec". Given that the company does not receive drawings from the clients, it needs to make a product that has zero problems, so that there is no room for malfunctions. In case the product does not work, two developments could cause the company to crash ☐ first, if customers perceive the product to be of inherently poor quality and spread the word telling others as much. This would lead to heavy monetary losses. Second, in many countries, consumer protection laws require that the customers' payment be refunded, in which case the company would have to issue a recall on the malfunctioning product, and heavy losses would follow.

Quality control in a product-based company is based on what the product should do. For example, in products combining electronics and plastics, quality control examines not only the parameters of each component, but also the combination of the two. The functionality test checks the product against what the product is supposed to do and it is conducted by an independent quality control department, so that production constraints have no effect on product examination. The quality control department operates according to a specific, predetermined format, so as to examine the product in terms of every anticipated scenario that might occur throughout the lifespan of the product. When dealing with products that are extremely complex in terms of expected scenarios, the quality testing is done superficially on most of the products in a batch, so as not to increase production costs substantially, and only a few randomly selected units undergo the full cycle of tests. This is sufficient to ensure that the product can withstand the maximal loads anticipated during its life cycle.

As shown in previous chapters, product-based companies develop brands, in which they typically invest large sums of money. A single sloppily produced product can cause enough damage to close down the company, thus forfeiting everything invested in creating the brand. Toyota, for example, one of the major brands in the car industry, suffered a severe blow to its reputation when the American media announced that the gas pedal in one of the company's models was faulty. Better investment in quality control could have prevented this event. If a product-based company is forced to recall its products every few months due to some technical malfunction or other, not only does it have to absorb the fiscal loss, but also the blow to the company's image.

A famous case in Israel in which quality control failure led to the closing of a product-based company was that of

Remedia. The Israeli Remedia company was the second most important player in the market of baby formula products. In late October of 2003, various hospitals reported emergency cases of babies presenting with neurological symptoms such as apathy, seizures etc. On Wednesday, November 5, 2003 four babies remained in the Schneider Children Hospital with severe neurological damage due to an unknown cause. After examination, it was found that the only connection between them was that they had been fed with Remedia's non-milk-based baby formula. The Ministry of Health questioned the parents, and announced on Friday, November 7, that Remedia's Soy-based Super-Formula should not be used. It was found that the product lacked the essential B1 vitamin, the absence of which can lead to neurological deficiencies in infants, and even death. Three babies died as a result, and dozens suffered severe neurological impairment. Senior personnel in the company were charged with causing death by negligence, and the parents are still involved in a civil suit against the company. The State, in an unusual stance, brought similar charges also against Ministry of Health personnel who were responsible for checking new food compounds for children.

In this case, Remedia is a product-based company that failed to conduct proper quality testing on its products and, as a result, found itself in an unimaginable situation. You may think that this example demonstrates the importance of quality testing in a product-based company, where quality control ensures that the products meet all of the required standards. Quite so – but here the plot thickens. The example also validates the paradigm theory regarding the categories of manufacturing, product-based and solutions-based companies. In the Remedia[6] story, the manufacturer of the formula was the German company Humana. Humana's major function is as a product-based brand name company. It served as the manufacturer solely for Remedia's Soy-based Super Formula, which it delivered, along with the quality test results, to the Israeli Remedia company, for marketing in Israel. For a reason that remains unclear, there was a failure in the process of testing for the values of B1 vitamin at Humana, so that the results obtained were significantly higher than the actual amount of the vitamin in the product. In this case, since Humana served only as the manufacturing company it has not been sued (until now) for its share in this matter (although it is possible that Remedia will sue after it receives its verdict). Had the product been marketed under the Humana brand when failure this occurred, it is likely that the Humana company would have had to close down, as happened to Remedia, since it is

---

[6] http://www.ynetnews.com/articles/0,7340,L-4344508,00.html

always the product-based company and not the manufacturing company that is responsible towards customers, in this case the parents and the Ministry of Health.

The Remedia case highlights the importance of quality control in a product-based company in contrast to a manufacturing company. In a solutions-based company, quality control should be even stricter. Returning to Remedia, effectively, the company was sued because the B1 content in the product did not coincide with what was written on the package label. Legally, it is conceivable that if the package had noted the actual values of B1 with an announcement that B1 should be added to the formula, it would not have been held liable for what happened to the children. In this example, it was the gap between what was declared on the product and the actual content which caused the company to close. However, according to the paradigm introduced here, it is my claim that parents that purchase a baby formula expect a complete solution for their baby's nutrition. A company such as Remedia should realize it is offering more than a product; it is responsible for the solution as well. Given the function of the product, the company could not afford to depend on the parents to give the correct dose of vitamins to their infants. Therefore, even a warning on the package would not have relieved the company of its responsibility. Being perceived as a solutions provider means the company has to work harder to meet more rigorous standards, including the clients' expectations, even if these do not coincide with the writing on the package.

The responsibility of a solutions-based company is much greater than that of a product-based company. As mentioned, by marketing its product, a product-based company takes responsibility for the product's ingredients and its functioning, unlike a solutions-based company, which that takes responsibility for the results of using the product. Therefore, quality control in a solutions-based company includes not only the ingredients and functioning of the product; in this case, quality control has to ascertain that the product's use leads to the desired results.

A famous example is the example of the Israeli product Mega-Gluflex, produced by Ta'am-Teva–Altman. According to the company's ads, the product helps rebuild and restoring cartilage in addition to reducing joint pains. In 2006, a class action was brought against the company, claiming that the product does not restore cartilage and does not assist in curing the disease that led to cartilage erosion. It only helps alleviate the pain. Even an expert on behalf of the company claimed "we are still unable to cure the disease, only reduce the symptoms".

The judge, Magen Altuvia wrote: "it appears that all agree that the product is unable to cure the disease… I believe that the reasonable customer coming upon the claims of the defendant as a whole might be misled into thinking that not only can use of the product relieve pains, but also 'solve the problem from the inside' as the ad implies, in other words, cure the illness". Thus, the judge understood that by trying to sell a solution rather than a product, the company was effectively misleading the customer. The company's slogan was "Mega-Gluflex – because the body doesn't come with spare parts". In its ad, it told customers it was selling a solution that can fight cartilage erosion. The judge, who understood that the company advertisements claimed to offer a solution rather than a product, rejected the company's claims that since the product contained ingredients that brought relief to patients and thus improved their quality of life it should be considered legitimate product. During the course of the trial it was clear to all that the pills do alleviate patients' pain, and many users of the product testified as much. In fact, the trial revolved around the question whether the company sold a solution or a product. Had the company not claimed to sell a solution, it would not have been sued, because there was no doubt that the product was effective in reducing pain caused by cartilage erosion. The company's problem began when it decided to sell solutions to the customer, without fully understanding the implications of such a decision.

Thus, selling a solution has advantages and as well as drawbacks. The major advantage is the ability to charge a higher price for the product, since this is not just a pain-reducer, but provides also a general solution to the illness. However, the drawback is that the product must in fact work as a solution. After the lawsuit, the company withdrew the advertisement promising the clients a solution, as it understood that it was not actually solving their problem.

A company that sells a solution cannot be satisfied with quality control of the components of the product; it needs to examine the quality of the solution offered. The quality of the solution includes the solutions mentioned in the company advertisements, and also those the client expects, even if not explicitly mentioned or advertised. Quality control of service-based solutions, e.g., transportation, hospitality or medical or communication services, could be the examination of the percentage of trains that are late, customer satisfaction among hotel guests, time spent in the doctor's waiting room, or the level of cellular reception anywhere in the country. Interestingly, all of these examples are features that the clients themselves could not easily test, which in turn makes it nearly impossible to sue solutions-based companies. Nevertheless, court-ridden or not, a company that offers a solution that does not meet the standards expected by the client simply cannot survive.

To summarize, in

- Manufacturing companies – quality control requires minimal testing time. As soon as the prototype adheres to the physical specifications set by the client, it is passed on to the customer for approval and beginning of production.

- Production-based companies – quality control testing requires more time, and focuses on the product's components and functionality. Does the product work as expected, without a problem?

- Solutions-based companies – quality control testing is a prolonged process, since it entails examination over time, to determine whether the solution indeed addresses the problem sufficiently.

Service

People are prepared to pay more in return for good service, as the shops full of customers will attest. Often, customers who could find and purchase products on the Internet prefer to buy those same products at a store --even though they might be charged more, because they feel more confident about their purchase when they can see who they buy from, and know where to go if they want to return or exchange the product. Service is one of the factors the potential customer considers when deciding whether to purchase one product over another. Customers expect someone to take responsibility for the product, and to have a place where they can address their complaints in case they encounter any problems.

In referring to service, I do not mean the purchasing experience, which will be analyzed separately, but rather the service provided after the purchase has been made. In a buyer's world, where "the customer is always right", service is a major issue.

There are two types of service: Service that is provided following a complaint, and service initiated by the company. Both types are crucial for the success of the business, but they have different implications in terms of the customer's perspective and perception of the company.

Companies are aware that a customer is ready to accept that fact that mishaps may occur, that mistakes can happen and are forgivable if the seller operates in good faith and the company is prepared to take full responsibility and compensate for the damages. Problems arise if a company refuses to compensate the customer, because of the cost involved. This leads to an inevitable clash between customer and company. Companies can emerge from such encounters with a stronger brand image, if they respond by providing good service; in contrast, companies that failed to deal with a crisis to the customers' satisfaction have been known to flounder.

In a manufacturing company, there is a simple expectation: "Produce this according to the drawing and on time"; therefore, in a manufacturing company, if these demands are met, no additional service should be necessary.

However, problems begin in times of pressure, if the client fails to submit the drawings and specifications in a timely fashion, or if some of the instructions are unclear. Any one of these situations can steer the project timeline off course, which inevitably leads to customer dissatisfaction.

Often a manufacturing company may accept a job knowing full well that the timeline for production is tight, but finds handling the constraints preferable to losing a customer to the competition. Yet the cost of failing to meet the client's expectations can be just as high. In a manufacturing company, where management is scarce and already working at full capacity, the need to handle client complaints becomes an expensive burden. In addition, given that the profit margin in such companies is relatively narrow, providing monetary compensation in the form of a significant discount to a dissatisfied customer is a disagreeable prospect. The advantage for a manufacturing company is that expectations are not high, and because the clients are themselves large companies, they usually are aware that the same could happen even if they were to work with a different manufacturer. A large client takes into consideration that the company might not be able to produce the supply on time, and so if the delay is reasonable, disappointment is unlikely.

In contrast to the tolerance clients may show in relation to supply times, they do not tolerate problems related to the quality of the product. A manufacturing company that furnishes a product different than the one on the drawing will not be paid and, moreover, is likely to be sued for damages. Therefore, manufacturing companies --if forced to choose ☐ will prefer to deliver the product later than schedules, but to adhere to the client's specifications for the product.

In a product-based company, service is a major consideration in the customer's decision to choose a specific product, and it is definitely a significant factor in the pricing of the product. A product-based company plans a faultless product, knowing that any problem could lead to complete profit loss. Product-based companies are aware that the customers are sophisticated and demanding. If customers find a product faulty, at the very least they will return it to the shop and expect full remuneration. Shop owners usually have agreements with suppliers, so the cost of the return is on the supplier. This means that a manufacturer that refuses to accept the return of faulty products will find that no shop is willing to carry that product. The high cost of flaws in production leads to two combined results: The first, mentioned in the previous chapter, is the need to maintain strict quality control standards and to test all products leaving the company, in order to preclude any need for repairs; and the second is the need to operate special service departments to placate dissatisfied clients. The level of service in a product-based company can sometimes reach an absurd level, whereby a customer who complains of the quality of the product is compensated at a sum that far exceeds that of the initial purchase. This is often done without even examining the product to ascertain that it in fact faulty. This is true in the case of food manufacturers. A customer claiming that the product purchased tastes off or contains a foreign object is automatically (after checking that this is not a serial petitioner) compensated, most often with coupons valued at five to ten times the cost of the original product.

The reason behind this compensation is the company's understanding that a customer left dissatisfied will broadcast this fact to everyone around, including over the Internet. A dissatisfied customer can have a much greater effect than one hundred satisfied ones. This can cause grave damage to the company's image; therefore, product-based companies opt to invest in customer service departments, and work hard to placate their customers to the best of their ability.

Product-based companies also invest in proper training on the use of the product, so that customers can maximize their pleasure from the product and its abilities. The purpose of training is not marketing, but preventing future complaints, thus converting potential complaining customers into satisfied customers who recommend the product. A customer who has been trained in the use of a given product has deeper and more emotional ties to the product, and thus is worth more to the company than a "lukewarm" customer, who has not received training. An additional purpose of the training is to prevent damage to the product, which would then be followed by a complaint and, consequently, the need for high-cost compensation.

Training has many faces: It may simply be a page of instructions attached to the product, or in more advanced cases, it may be in the form of detailed written instructions on the Internet, complemented by pictures and even a video tutorial. The highest level of training is when a representative of the company is sent to the client's premises to conduct personal training. This takes place only in the case of expensive products, but the results justify the expense. The client feels an affiliation with the company and is grateful to it for the training received.

A solutions-based company is committed to an even higher level of service, because of the emotional and often dependent ties with the customers. When the network of the Israeli cellular communication company, Cellcom, crashed for twenty-four hours, the clients reacted as if lives were at stake. Their responses and the media's reaction suggested that the effect of the event was tantamount to a natural disaster. The company managed the crisis by holding a press conference, and invested millions in a speedy repair of the problem. The company offered compensation within twenty-four hours, even before there was any decision on the class action taken against it. It declared zero charges for calls and text messages dating from **one week before** the problem occurred, although the failure lasted only 24 hours. In other word, compensation was seven-fold that of the alleged damage to the client. Indeed, most clients incurred no damages at all, as they were able to communicate via another supplier. The solutions-based company's purpose in offering such disproportionate compensation is to convey the message to clients that it is ready to do whatever it takes ☐ indeed anything it takes ☐ to prevent them from taking their business elsewhere..

Service in a solutions-based company can also be provided face-to-face. This does not happen usually in a product-based company. In a solutions-based company, the client is able to meet a company representative, rather than place a call and have the complaint handled by a call center representative who recites preset texts. The personal relationship is important for building trust between the client and the firm. This relationship is indeed crucial in companies that encourage clients to blindly place their trust in the company.

In a solutions-based company, the service accompanies the whole life span of the solution, not just a certain period after purchase. In a product-based company, a warranty is given for a specific period, usually between one to three years. This warranty period is quite meaningless, since it covers only damages to the product that occurred prior to delivery, and it refrains from covering any damage resulting from use. Therefore, such a warranty is typically implemented within a short while after purchase. Later, the percentage of customers filing for warranty coverage is small. In a solutions-based company, the service is continuous, throughout the use of the product. There are two reasons for this: The client views the purchase as an on-going process. In addition, the company too has a need to maintain on-going contact with its customers, so as to obtain feedback on the solution, to hear customers' opinions, concerns and suggestions for additional solutions. By providing ongoing service, the company also gains continuous access to the clients and can build a useful relationship. Service becomes a way in which the company incorporates customers into the firm's development team and then remunerates them for their input regarding the product's quality and design

To summarize, in

- Manufacturing companies – service means supplying the product per specification and on time.
- Product-based companies – service means customer support and compensation in case of a problem, as well as training when appropriate..

- Solutions-based companies – service takes the form of an on-going relationship with the client, to examine responses to problems and receive continuous feedback about the solution. In case of a failure, compensation is significant.

Warranty

Service is an outcome of the warranty that a firm provides for its product. This warranty is usually defined in writing, and constitutes part of any purchase transaction. The form and the period of warranty vary by company, but the basis is identical – a warranty promises that upon leaving the company, the product was in proper functional condition. The warranty is usually limited in time, to avoid future monetary damages and to induce clients to purchase new products from the company after the old ones have stopped working.

Warranty actually defines the product's lifespan for the client. A client who has paid for a certain product with a three-year warranty does not expect to have to buy the same product again for the next three years. Therefore, the issue of a warranty ensures the customers of future service; however, it also constitutes a marketing decision for the company, as it is one of the factors that customers consider before purchasing a product.

Some companies offer a life-warranty for their products, such as the lighter company Zippo, or the Lowe Alpine pack manufacturer. Lately the British car company Vauxhaul advertised[7] that its cars would come with a life-time warranty (or up to 100,000 miles). Almost all companies limit the life-warranty by certain conditions, but the very fact that such a warranty exists provides them with an enormous marketing advantage, and a reliable image relative to that of their competitors.

In a manufacturing company, the warranty is very limited. The client dictates what ingredients should be used and how to produce the specific product. Therefore, if the product is done according to specifications but breaks after a short period of use, the client has no one else to blame but himself. The manufacturing company does not offer any warranty on the products it makes: As soon as the client has

---

[7] http://www.vauxhall.co.uk/owners_services/warranty_assistance/vauxhall_life time_warranty.html

reviewed the product, found it satisfactory and signed the product acceptance form, the manufacturing company has no liability for the product, and the client assumes all the responsibility. If after leaving the factory, a product is found to be faulty, it cannot be returned to the manufacturer (except in special specified cases, or if the statistical checks missed a flaw that was found to occur repeatedly).

In a product-based company, the warranty is part of the product, not an external addition. When a product is purchased, it is expected to serve the customer for a certain minimal period, during which coverage is warranted. A customer would never buy a product thinking it might disintegrate within a month's time. The warranty is in fact the firm's declaration that the product will work for a predefined amount of time. If within this period the product becomes faulty, the company understands it has to fix it, since this is part of the agreement with the customer.

A firm's credibility is measured by the warranty provided. In product-based companies, the warranty phase begins once the company receives the payment for the purchase. Therefore, only reliable companies that intend to stay on the market for an extended period agree to repair or replace the product at no additional cost. Less reliable firms that wish to make a quick profit and disappear refuse to provide a warranty, so as not to undertake a costly expense that has no advantage in the framework in which they operate.

In a solutions-based company, the solution comes with a life-time guarantee. This is exactly what the customer has agreed to pay for – a long-term result. The warranty here is not on the product but on its ability to provide a solution to a specific problem. This shifts the total responsibility to the company, even for the choice of the product. A cellular company is prepared to replace a client's phone at no cost, not only when the phone does not work, but also if the particular model of phone gets no reception in the area where the customer lives. A solutions-based company does not usually provide a warranty for the product or for the conditions stipulated in the customer's contract; rather, it guarantees the functioning of the whole operations environment. That's why you can find cellular companies that spend a lot of money installing a new communications system if the old one is over-loaded, or if an external obstacle appears, such as a newly erected building that blocks reception to a certain type of apparatus or in a certain area.

To summarize, in

- Manufacturing companies – the warranty entails adhering to the client's specifications, namely, that the product is manufactured according to the materials described at the quality defined. There is no long-term warranty.

- Product-based companies – the warranty covers the product's functionality, it promises that the product will do what it is supposed to do over a predetermined period of time.

- Solutions-based companies – the warranty is for the final outcome. Even if the product leaves the plant without any fault, but does not provide the client with the desired solution or usage experience, the company will compensate the customer and provide another product that is able to produce the desired solution.

International Marketing

Nowadays, international marketing is a basic necessity for most companies, but the precise demands and characteristics of this marketing change according to the company's category and focus.

As mentioned earlier, manufacturing companies rely mostly on their greatest advantage, namely, their location, which translates into cost-effective production and the ability to better compete in the market. At the same time, this dictates the need to engage in intensive international marketing. The international marketing efforts of a manufacturing company promote the company's production abilities and its reliability. The main challenge that manufacturers face is create a window of opportunity, by convincing potential clients from developed countries to give their company a try. The underlying assumption is that a satisfied client will choose to continue to work with the same manufacturer; therefore, manufacturing companies tend to go a long way to ensure the customer is satisfied, even if it means investing a great deal just to fill a small order.

Let me share again an example from my own experience. In the process of developing engines for wind turbines, I needed to purchase magnets with certain qualities. I searched for manufacturing companies on the international trade site named Alibaba and sent out numerous requests to various candidates asking for a price quote for these magnets. I received an astonishing number of replies, representing a wide range of prices. Each company had a website and each sent me background material with explanations about its size and experience in this area.

I could not figure out which one was better than the rest. From here they all looked the same to me. It took me time to cross check the price quotes, and I ran some technical tests, but in the process I realized that although all of the companies maintained that they were manufacturing companies, only about half of them actually were manufacturers. The other half, simply bought products from manufacturers and marketed them to the customers, basically taking advantage of the fact that due to their distant location I (and presumably other potential customers) had no way of knowing this – other than spending a great deal of time to thoroughly investigate each and every one of them, which in fact I did. This is precisely the reason that true manufacturing companies need to gain the trust of their potential clients and convince them of the company's ability to do the required job. With a major portion of the potential clientele located in foreign and often distant countries, characterized by a diversity of cultures and mentalities, there is clearly a need to place a representative on the target location in order to build trust.

The effort to convince a foreign client that your company is reliable must be multiplied many times over when marketing through the Internet. Many manufacturers cannot afford to travel to meet each potential overseas customer, as that expense would have to be added on to the cost, thus eliminating their pricing advantage. Consequently, online marketing is the preferred vehicle for many manufacturers, who attempt to prove their reliability by posting photos of their production lines, inviting prospects to visit their production sites, and gaining the approval of large B2B companies such as Alibaba (for example, by being awarded the status of "Gold Supplier").

Now that we have established that it is critically important for manufacturing companies to maintain an international presence, let us consider the case of product-based companies and the degree of international exposure that they require.

In this regard, the case of product-based companies is more complex than that of manufacturing companies. In the latter, we have noted that the majority of the work comes from client companies in other countries. The criterion of location plays a role – albeit a more complex one – also for product-based companies. Thus, I suggest that product-based companies originating in consumer or developed countries differ from product-based companies from manufacturing or developing countries. Clearly, this way of defining countries is not clear-cut, and one cannot precisely characterize a country as being only one and not the other. Nevertheless, the reason for drawing this line is to show that product-based companies behave differently according to their country of origin, and more precisely, according to the consumers' behavior in that location. In manufacturing countries, the customers seek to buy branded products from consumer countries, while in consumer countries there is hardly any demand for brands from manufacturing countries.

Let us take the Coca-Cola brand as an example. The Coca-Cola Company has a global presence and the rate of its recognition is over 97%: The entire world population is familiar with the Coca-Cola brand. By contrast, no one in the US is aware of Future Cola, the strongest Chinese brand after Coca-Cola and Pepsi. There are two interrelated reasons for this distinction between the products. The first is the brand and its implied values. People in developing countries want to resemble their counterparts from developed countries, and therefore they prefer to buy a brand identified with a developed country. The inverse is also true: People in developed countries do not trust products from developing countries, and have no interest in using an unfamiliar brand.

The second reason, which is closely related to the first, is the actual quality of the products. In developing countries, a brand from a developed country does not need to compete for its place on the market in terms of price, but in terms of quality. It is clear to a customer in a developing country that a branded product from a developed country is more expensive and of higher quality than a local brand. At the same time, the local product-based company in a developing country must be competitive in terms of price, in order to maintain its place on the market. Consequently, the quality of the product – or, at the very least, as it is perceived by customers – is lesser than that of the foreign brand. This is the reason why brands from developing countries find it almost impossible to penetrate the markets of developed countries. The brand from the developing country is unknown, and therefore it is considered to be of lesser quality. As a result, large product-based companies of developing countries seek to buy the rights to brand names from developed countries, in order to get a foothold in the markets of developing countries. Examples abound in this area, starting from Lenovo that bought the IBM laptop market, to Tata, which purchased the brands Rover and Jaguar.

A product-based company from a developed country may choose to manufacture its products in a developing country, so as to save on production costs. From there it is easy to market the products in the same manufacturing country and in the neighboring countries, in addition to selling in its home location. Thus, the international marketing of a product-based company from a developed country is usually aided by its use of a foreign manufacturer and by leveraging its well-grounded brand name.

Consider the case of an Israeli chain that sells soap, which based on its unique expertise as well as the high quality of its products, was able to expand its market into additional countries, such as Japan and Germany. As the company grew, its ability to penetrate foreign markets improved, and thus it entered more markets and used the

Internet to fortify the brand name. As a product-based company from a developing country, it had to work much harder to find its way into developed countries and establish an international market than would a company from a developed company. To begin with, the difficulty stems from gaps in image and mentality. A product-based company from a developing country has to compete with stronger international players in its own local market, and therefore it must learn to make simple products at cheap prices. Yet upon bringing these same products into developed countries, where the well-known motto is "you can't afford to buy cheap products", the company encounters a different type of clientele, where customers almost always prefer to pay a little more for a product of higher quality. Of course, product-based companies from developing countries are very interested in penetrating the markets of developed countries, since the profit margins they can obtain for their products are much higher there than in their own countries. To achieve the goal of penetrating into the market of developed countries, the product needs to be of an even higher quality than the products already available in the developed countries; thus, the local consumers in developed countries might think that although the product is from such-and-such a place, its quality is truly unique. This means that the product must adhere to the basic international standards and, in order to succeed, it needs to be superior to its competitors on the market in terms of the finished quality.

Product-based companies do not require international physical presence. They can operate through local distributors in various countries, under concessions or any other model. In this way, management expenses and cultural gaps are reduced, as is the risk entailed in any attempt to penetrate a new market.

International marketing of a product-based company from a developing country involves a different strategy from that available to a company from a developed country. While the latter, assuming it has a high quality product and a familiar brand name, can select its representatives from a pool of interested candidates in the destination country, the former will need more than that to obtain equal footing. A company from a developing country must work much harder to convince potential customers that its product is suited to the developed market and that it has plans to continue the brand's development over time. The reason for this of course is the fact that traditionally, product-based companies from developing countries actually did offer lower quality products to their local markets in order to compete --at least as far as price is concerned-- against similar products from developing countries. However, unlike the case in their local markets, in the international market the difference in price is not enough to provide a competitive edge. Indeed, to compete with internationally renowned brands, these product-based companies from developing countries must be able to compete also in terms of the quality of the product. The best way for a company to demonstrate its ability to compete in terms of product quality is to start selling the product in the local (developing country's) market but at a higher price, similar to that of the international brand's product. Thus, the local market can serve as a test ground: If the local customers in a developing country prefer the local brand to the foreign one even though the price is the same for both products, then the local product is probably of sufficient quality to compete in the international arena.

In a solutions-based company, not surprisingly, the situation is even more complicated. A solutions-based company cannot be international in the same way that product-based companies are. In other words, it cannot sell the same product in different markets. It needs to provide different solutions to different clients in different countries. While it most likely aims to address the same needs in foreign countries as in the local market, the solutions offered must have different characteristics.

Solutions-based companies use their accumulated knowledge and their unique capabilities to open branches and subsidiaries in other countries; yet they have to invest a lot of time and money to study the target market and adapt the solutions to that specific market. These companies do not use distributors or concessionaires in the countries they wish to penetrate; they understand that without a physical presence in these countries they will fail. If they need a local person or entity, or if the country's regulations demand they take on a local partner, they do so; however, it is always the solutions-based company that delineates the local company's policy.

There are many examples of solutions-based companies that have succeeded in establishing a global presence; however, the complexities entailed in the international marketing of such companies can best be observed in the case of insurance companies. Insurance companies have a specific incentive for expanding internationally, as this expansion allows them to disperse the risk among many geographical locations. At the same time, the products they offer differ from one location to the next. Thus, a company that sells a policy insuring against earthquakes and abductions will probably offer a different product combination in Japan than in Angola, presumably with a greater emphasis on earthquakes in the former and a product with the inverse ratio in the latter location. Another concern of the insurance company would be to have agents capable of gaining the trust of the population, which entails recruiting and hiring local personnel for the sales and marketing departments. The issue of local regulation of insurance companies is yet another potentially complicating factor. Occasionally, the country's regulations require the founding of a local company, but in any case, the preference would be to hire local experts who know how to work with the country's regulating body.

Thus, solutions-based companies that wish to succeed in a market other than their own must invest a great deal in order to open a branch, at the very least, if not a unique company, capable of fulfilling all of the functions of the home company. To market in the international arena, they must leverage their brand name and use their unique knowledge, but they cannot transfer any of the manufacturing or operational advantages which they enjoy in their home market to the international setting.

To summarize, for international marketing to succeed,

- Manufacturing companies – must focus on convincing potential clients to rely on them.

- Product-based companies – from developed countries must find distributors with relevant ties to clients or shops that sell synergistic or competing products. Product-based companies from developing countries have to prove to distributors that the quality of their products is sufficient to compete in the international market. The best way to prove this is to successfully compete in their home markets against international name brands, and thus facilitate the move to the international arena.

- Solutions-based companies – must establish a subsidiary or a branch in the foreign markets of their choice, adapt the solution to the characteristics of the local clientele, and build a sense of trust and reliability with their clients.

Presence on the Internet

As shown in the previous chapter, Internet presence is crucial for manufacturing companies' ability to progress. Manufacturing companies use the Internet for two purposes: marketing and receiving information related to the production work. These companies must be establish their presence on the Internet both by establishing a multilingual Website that describes the company's capabilities, and by registering their site with all of the search engines and with professional index sites, such as *Alibaba* or B2B, where clients may go to look for a manufacturing company. Sites are an important component in the production company's ability to advance and develop.

Currently, most manufacturing companies do not use the Internet in ways that sufficiently demonstrate their professional expertise. The problem does not necessarily lie with the manufacturing companies themselves but rather, it is due to the thousands of mediators posing as manufacturers, which makes it difficult to distinguish the site of a manufacturing company from that of a mediating company. A possible solution would be to post a list of satisfied clients; however, one of the greatest obstacles in this case is that most often clients wish to maintain their anonymity. Another possible solution for providing proof on the Internet is by placing cameras within the company that are broadcast online to the manufacturer's Website, so that the company can distinguish itself from the thousands copycats. In addition, companies can provide details regarding the types of machines they have and operate as well as answers to technical questions online. This can help clients know that the company is indeed professional. Another possible solution is establishing an entity that can ascertain that a firm is in fact a manufacturer; yet this approach is rather cumbersome and is liable to be problematic, as there will always be those who will try to imitate the examining entity.

Without an impressive Internet presence, product-based companies today cannot support a brand and maintain its values. Product-based companies must support their product on the Internet and use the Website's homepage to provide all the relevant information about the company. By opening a page on the social networks, the company lets the product assume a life of its own on the net. Product-based companies must take care also to write favorable talkbacks on articles or forums that mention their product, and sometimes it's also necessary to disparage the competition. The Internet is an environment where every product must vie for positive attention and assume a life of its own. Typically, a potential customer would examine the product, find out how other users feel about it, and use sites specializing in product comparison to understand the advantages and limitations of the various options. A product without Internet presence has a very small chance of surviving on the market – not to mention succeeding.

The challenge of the Internet is crucial to all product-based companies, but even more critical to companies attempting to penetrate a new category, which is already ruled by dominant players. A new product-based company needs to use the net to create positive feedback for the product and to showcase its abilities at a low cost. A number of clips on a video-sharing site such as YouTube, using an innovative twist to present the product's abilities, can induce the viewer to recommend the product to others. This type of recommendation is worth more than primetime advertising on TV. Thus, for example, a blender company[8] seeking to gain exposure bought Apple's newest iPhone and iPad models on the very day they entered the market, and ground them in the blender. The video and the company had more viewers and attention than any other regular advertiser at that time. The ability to create a large campaign using a small budget, enhanced by word of mouth, changes the playing field for product-based companies. If at one time, in order to become a dominant player on the market, the company had to invest large sums in advertising, marketing and physical access to the shops, currently the same effect may be obtained by creating an original campaign with a good shop on the Internet.

In solutions-based companies, the Internet does not only serve for marketing, but is mainly another layer in the solution provided to the client. A solutions-based company whose solution is not presented on the Internet eventually will fail to provide an overall solution. The amount of time people spend on the Internet is such that customers expect any product and certainly any solution to be available there.

---

[8] http://www.willitblend.com/

An example of a solution on the Internet may be the ability to send text messages from the cellular company's

site, or the ability to see and access one's bank account online. Another type of solution is one that collects information from the net and brings it to the client in an organized fashion and at the time required, or similarly, collects information regarding Internet trends to help identify the solution the client wants or needs.

Some solutions-based companies provide solutions on the Internet, as in human resource companies, or firms that enable you to detect the location of your car, or ones that find the most relevant sites for what you are looking for. The Internet is an important and necessary tool for a solutions-based company, and it must include this resource as part of the solution. A product-based company that wishes to become a solutions provider can also do so through the Internet. For example a company that sells portable phones can supply additional services through the Internet, such as the ability to download games, ask questions about the tools and other issues, and in this manner it can provide its clients a perfect solution to their problems.

To summarize,

MANUFACTURING, PRODUCT, SOLUTIONS

- Manufacturing companies - need limited exposure on professional sites, in order to be found by potential clients seeking a supplier.

- Product-based companies – must use the Internet as a means to support the product, creating presence and promoting the product via social networks, talkbacks and recommendations.

- Solutions-based companies – use the Internet as an additional component of the solution, operating under the assumption that the Internet is the medium most available to the client.

The Sales Team

I dedicate a chapter to the sales team because essentially it represents the image of the company, that is, the company as it would like to be perceived.

The sales team in a manufacturing company works within the market of government and local institutions. Usually sales team members have had experience working in the market to which they are assigned, which helps them talk to clients on equal terms and convince them to give the job to the company they represent. The main mission of sales representatives is to bring in the potential client and trust them one hundred percent to do the job properly. In a manufacturing company, the sales reps' remuneration is often based on the volume of orders they bring in. Thus, they are rewarded for their ability to bring in orders, which in turn guarantee that the company will be able to issue their paychecks at the end of the month.

In a manufacturing company, representing the company's image is not a priority for the sales personnel. A manufacturer is by default considered an expert in the given field, so that there is no need to glamorize this fact; therefore, the sales people need to be accessible and affable. If potential customers find the sales people's approach elitist, they will assume that these representatives are not genuinely acquainted with the manufacturing world and will not entrust them with their orders.

In a product-based company, usually sales people work with stores and distributors. Their aim is to make the client believe that the merchandise ordered will sell like hotcakes. Members of the sales team of a product-based company don't need to have an in-depth understanding of the product they sell; they need to understand the mindset of the trader they face. Product sales people study the basic data about the product, in order to be able to convince potential clients that the product is worthwhile, and that there will be demand for it on the market. They must appear professional, in order to convey that the company is serious, and has the capacity to back the product. This is essential if they are to win the trust of potential clients. If a product fails to work properly, even if the company bears all the return costs and the vendor does not incur significant monetary loss, it is eminently clear that the vendor or distributor's reputation will suffer. Therefore, sales people must project reliability and professionalism. In product-based companies, sales people earn a certain percentage of their total sales, which motivates them to increase the volume of sales as much as possible.

In a solutions-based company, members of the sales team need to be experts in their fields. They have to explain to the client the problem, and how it can best be solved. In this case, the sales people often remain in touch with clients over a period of time, so as to ensure the customers' satisfaction with the solution received. In a solutions-based company, the sales reps' remuneration is linked directly to clients' payments. Thus, for example, in the case of an insurance company, a certain percentage of the clients' premium payments go to the agent/sales person. The objective of the sales person in a solutions-based company is to ensure the clients' satisfaction over time, so that the clients continue to pay for the solution. If sales reps' remuneration were not linked to clients' payments, but took the form of a one-time bonus per client, the solutions-based company would run the risk of sales people bringing in clients for whom the solution is unsuitable, in an effort prioritize quantity over quality. Therefore the payment is continuous, as is the nature of the solution.

To summarize, in

- Manufacturing companies – there is a small number of sales people, who are experts in their field, and whose remuneration is linked to the volume of work they bring in.

- Product-based companies – there is a need for a large number of sales people, who usually do not fully understand the product's workings, but have the skills to persuade a potential client to buy almost anything. Remuneration is linked to the volume of sales.

- Solutions-based companies – the sales people have an in-depth understanding of the client's problem, and remuneration is linked to the client's payments over time, which are considered a sign of the client's satisfaction and support for the product.

Marketing Icons

Every company has a few clients who have their own followers. These are known as strategic clients. In the best case scenario, they receive significant discounts; otherwise, the company pays them to use its products. In the consumer products market, these clients are known as line-of-business influencers, and in the institutional market they are called "anchor clients". These are existing clients, who attract the company of other potential clients, who in turn opt to follow suit and become clients of the same company.

Every company knows it is harder to sell the first product rather than the thousandth. Enlisting the first paying customer is often the greatest hurdle for a company, and a significant milestone in its history.

The challenge for manufacturing companies is greater than for the other company types. A manufacturing company needs to convince another firm that it can do the job, while maintaining the required quality and adhering to the required time schedule. A potential customer does not want to spend time or risk the company's reputation with a manufacturer that is unknown and possibly unable to do the work properly. Therefore, in order to recruit the first client, a manufacturing company is often prepared to take nearly desperate steps. Frequently, the first client is someone with whom the company owners already have a personal, trusting relationship. In return for trusting the new manufacturer with the product, this first customer is offered a handsome discount. A manufacturing company that cannot rely on a personal relationship may very well do the first job at no cost, or at a highly reduced price. In this manner, the client's risk is minimized, and the job gets done. If the client is satisfied with the outcome, additional paid orders will follow. The marketing icons of a manufacturing company are large-scale, satisfied companies that agree to disclose their professional relationship with the manufacturer and recommend its services to others. One such a client may be all that the manufacturer needs to lure in additional new clients.

A product-based company has a larger number of clients than a manufacturing firm. Therefore, it prefers to use a famous figure as the company's line-of-business influencer. The effect of this influencer on potential customers, who identify with and as a result wish to emulate the user of the product, is stronger than any persuasive argument. Product-based companies that wish to appeal to the youth sector are willing to pay a pop star or a famous actor great sums of money to use and be photographed with their products. This strategy is extremely successful in making potential customers believe that the product is good for them and will make them look like the star.

A solutions-based company puts less emphasis on marketing icons and more on referral marketing, based on the satisfaction of the users. Marketing icons may give the solution a substantial boost in the initial stages. If the solution is in fact worthwhile, the relevant icons will opt to use it in any case; therefore, paying them to use the solution is a less relevant strategy. The effect of a friend's recommendation of a product is greater than that of a picture of a famous entity using that product. The objective of the solutions-based company is to provide such a perfect solution, that the clients will wonder how they ever managed before the solution was invented.

In the world of social networks, the demand for icons in general, and for solutions-based companies in particular, is greatly reduced. Companies today prefer to convince people with lots of online friends and contacts to use a certain product and write their review of the product on the social network. If the opinion is favorable, the effect on the other friends is enormous, and the rate of exposure for the new product is very high. In solutions-based companies, the emphasis on marketing through social networks is even greater, because if one person has a certain problem, it is conceivable that his or her friends are likely to have the same problem. The company's ability to solve the problem for one user, who then conveys this information to others, can bring the company more sales than any icon.

To summarize,

- Manufacturing companies – are proud to present large and well-known firms as their clients. In return for this testimony, the company offers the well-known firm a substantial discount on the first job.

- Product-based companies – They seek icons such as celebrities and opinion leaders to be shown with or using its products.

- Solutions-based companies – rely on their innovative solutions to attract those iconic figures who have the capacity to attract numerous others. The preferred strategy is referral marketing.

The Planning Horizon

After observing the differences between the various types of companies and their daily operations, we shall see how the company's self-concept affects its attitude towards the future.

The future refers to the period of time ahead, but the definition of planning for the future changes from one company to another.

In a manufacturing company, the future is quite near. The company needs to have a seasonal forecast of demands for its services, in order to prepare the raw materials and the personnel to fulfill the clients' demands. For example, a company specializing in producing parts for air conditioners knows that demand is fairly small in the winter, but rises towards summer, peaks at the beginning of summer and wanes towards the end of summer. Any company needs to be aware of patterns of market behavior, in order to be able to respond to the clients. If it is not prepared for the high-demand season, its clients will take their business elsewhere and never return. Therefore, the future in a manufacturing company is never far off. The company knows how to prepare itself for the following months, and tries to react to the market demands.

It may be said that planning in a manufacturing company is reactive rather than proactive. The company cannot create demand, only respond to the clients to the best of its ability, and continue to recruit additional clients. A manufacturing company does not affect the behavior of the end client. Therefore, if the market takes an unexpected turn, veering away from the field in which the company operates, the manufacturer is often usually the last to know. A company that discovers that the market no longer uses the products within its capability range is forced to buy new manufacturing technologies, in order to adjust to the new demands. In an optimistic scenario, timely notification will come from the manufacturer's clients, as they inquire about the company's ability to work with the new technology. Otherwise, if even the clients have not been able to recognize the evolving market trends, the clients themselves are apt to suffer financially, if they don't disappear off the map entirely.

A product-based company needs to make more careful and more long-term plans for the future, for a number of reasons. First, products should be ready and on the shelf as soon as there is demand; therefore, the company must make sure that the product has gone through the whole chain of production, packaging and supply. For example, a company that manufactures gift items must be ready for the week before Christmas, with its products in the shops, to be able to take advantage of the year's best week of sales. In addition, the company needs constantly to plan the next product to be introduced into the market. The company is aware that if it does not present clients with more advanced products, the competition will do so. In other words, the company must work constantly to improve its products. A product-based company usually plans its next two products based on its understanding of the market and the moves of the competition.

In addition, the product-based company needs to know clients' current interests as well as the direction in which they are headed, in order to market its products successfully. A company manufacturing school bags featuring children's television stars needs to know which programs and actors their target market considers attractive, so as to change the design on the product accordingly. Another parameter the company takes into account is the clients' desire to renew and advance, and the need to risk cannibalization of its own products rather than surrendering the market to competitors. Aware that clients will want to buy a newer and better product, the product-based company needs to be there, with the improved product already on the shelf. Companies need to alter their products with the advancement of technology; anyone that fails to understand this will disappear. The Kodak Company serves as an apt example: Failing to recognize the rise of digital photography, it lost not only its seniority in the market, but also suffered a nearly-devastating blow from which it has never fully recovered, as it remains a small and insignificant player in this market. The best indicator of its fall from glory was in 2004 when, for the first time in 72 years, it was removed from the Dow Jones Index.

Product-based companies plan their products for a range of two-three years, but cannot plan final products for a period greater than three years. The company's ability to forecast the state of the market beyond three years is so small, that any planning would likely become irrelevant.

Product-based companies do consider periods beyond the three year range, but not for the purpose of planning the products, but to foresee technological developments. The objective is to make products with the best technological advantages on the market. Therefore, their R&D

departments' technological development projects often exceed a period of three or five years. However, the move from technology to product requires much less. A company that possesses mature technology fit for a new product usually releases it within a year.

In a solutions-based company, the planning horizon always exceeds three years. The aim is to collect and select data that can help anticipate the clients' needs more than three years in advance. The ability of a solutions-based company to convince the client to use its solution is based almost solely on the ability to tell the client what developments to expect in the future as well as the likelihood of something happening at all, and this requires long-term planning. An insurance company, for example, can predict how many people will be killed in road accidents in the next five years; its biggest problem is that it cannot determine who. Planning, in solutions-based companies is based on continuously gathering data from clients. The larger their database, the greater and better their ability to foresee the future.

If, as seen, a manufacturing company is characterized by reactive planning, in an attempt to address technological developments on the market, and a product-based company plans in parallel to technological advancements, a solutions company is the trailblazer of technological change, as it delineates the direction of future progress for all other companies on the market.

A solutions-based company often selects a problem and begins to think of possible solutions, even before the market has acknowledged any need for a solution to that problem. Let's examine the differences between Apple and IBM regarding their perceptions of their place in the market. Apple produces amazing products, utilizing advanced technologies; nevertheless, its products use technologies that are well known on the market, albeit perfected by Apple to deliver a high level of convenience. In contrast, IBM takes huge challenges, which push the envelope of technological abilities, indicating the direction of progress for the rest of the industry. Processes such as the Deep-Blue chess playing computer, which in and of itself rendered little benefit to the world on the whole, yet its development added to the accumulated knowledge, pushing the world's computers to the next stage of development. Currently, IBM is working on a computer, known by the name of Watson[9], which has the capacity to play Jeopardy! and win. While there is little need in the world for this computer *per se*, but the abilities accumulated by IBM in developing

---

[9] http://researcher.ibm.com/researcher/view_project.php?id=2099

Watson will help solve thousands of problems, the existence – never mind the solution – of which we are probably unaware. The time range towards which Apple directs its development projects to span a period of about three years, whereas IBM has been working on Watson for six years already. As these lines are being written, it has been announced that "Watson will guide doctors on diagnoses and treatments" for cancer patients. Its ability to "process information from 200 million pages of literature in three seconds" enables it "to comb through patient medical histories, medical journals and clinical trials" and in this way assist physicians in the diagnosis and decision making processes.[10]

To summarize,

- Manufacturing companies –need to be able to foresee close-range, seasonal demands for its services, in order to prepare the required manpower and raw materials.

- Product-based companies – must work to improve their products in order to anticipate market demands and be ready before the competition is.

---

[10] Retrieved from http://articles.latimes.com/2011/dec/17/business/la-fi-cancer-computer-20111217 on December 18, 2011.

Based on sales estimates, the company produces for stock. It needs to be attentive to dramatic market changes that may make its products redundant.

- Solutions-based companies – examines the life habits of its clients and based on gathered data, it forecasts what they will need down the road. The planning horizon exceeds three years.

Regulation

Every company nowadays needs to cope with government regulations. Such regulations may be in the form of taxes or laws on the subject of labor, environmental protection or product standards.

In a manufacturing company, the coping with regulation mainly relates to defending employee rights and protecting the environment. These companies operate in a very competitive market, with low profit margins: Any increase in the employees' salaries is immediately apparent in the company's profit. While manufacturers strive to uphold labor laws in their countries, such laws sometimes fail to take into consideration that increasing employee benefits could impede the company's ability to compete on the international market, which could eventually lead to dismissals. Consequently, in countries in which the economy is based on production, regulations take into consideration the full range of concerns, including those of labor-intensive companies.

An additional factor, beyond regulation, which helps guarantee employee rights in production companies, is that of the clients, that is, the product-based companies and sometimes even the end-customers. Examples of this type of regulation include the commotion that arose in reaction to the rumors about the wave of suicides at Foxcon – a company that manufactures products for many notable electronics companies such as Apple, and the international protest that followed the publication of photos of small children sitting in rows and sewing shoes for Nike. Clients who refuse to purchase the products of a specific brand because of the attitude with which its suppliers treat their employees constitute the most effective regulation – consumer regulation – that can be imposed on manufacturing companies.

An additional regulation imposed on manufacturing companies is related to environmental protection. International awareness to environmental protection has increased over the past several years, so that even developing countries penalize foreign companies working within their territories for environmental damage. In environmental protection, there are also client organizations that disseminate information on the Internet regarding manufacturing companies, in an attempt to promote concern for environmental protection. For example, the Oreo Company produces cookies that contain palm oil, which it buys mainly from Indonesia. A rise of protests against the use of this oil, the production of which requires farmers to destroy tropical forests, have led Oreo to make sure that the oil it buys does not come from the extermination of rain forests that are habitats for orangutans. Thus, manufacturers need to adhere to local regulations to prevent cessation of production by the authorities.

In addition to regulations pertaining to employee rights and environmental protection, product-based companies need to adhere to both international and local legislation pertaining to the products it makes in each country. Consequently, many product-based companies have large legal departments and laboratories, the sole purpose of which is to prove to the authorities that the products they wish to market conform to local legislation. The objective of such legislation is to protect not only the users of the product, but also the local manufacturing companies. Local manufacturing companies are aware of the standardization instructions, but foreign companies or importers need to invest a great deal of effort to understand and adhere to these standards.

One of the main barriers preventing product-based companies from developing countries from penetrating the markets in developed countries is the need to adhere to International standards. Often foreign product-based companies find it difficult to understand the demands of international regulations. In addition, as mentioned in the chapter on international presence, a company that features simple products competes in its country of origin in terms of price; its ability to move to better products that compete on the quality parameter and meet all international regulations and standards is relatively limited.

In a solutions-based company, regulations often reach a high level, whereby the government enforces limitations on price, quality of service, availability of service, equal geographical distribution of the services, etc. The reason for such an extensive regulatory intervention is that once the public is accustomed to the idea that there is an immediate and accessible solution, it will expect to receive the same solution regardless of geographical location. For example, telephone companies are obliged by law to offer phone service at any point, and serve anyone interested in receiving their services. This is a governmental demand, despite the fact that it is often not economically feasible. Companies would gladly forego the provision of services in isolated locations. In addition, a solutions-based company that markets patent-based products must have a legal department capable of protecting the company's patents and preventing its being copied in any of the countries where the company operates.

In a solutions-based company, there is almost always a regulations department charged with dealing with legal issues and striving to alter the regulations to suit the company's needs.

To summarize, in

- Manufacturing companies – regulations pertain only to the functioning of the company in view of environmental and labor laws.

- Product-based companies – regulation includes also adhering to product standards.

- Solutions-based companies – regulations pertain to the service itself, including its availability and its equal distribution within a given jurisdiction.

In Lieu of a Summary

As seen in the book, the category to which a particular company fits determines numerous other aspects of its functioning. These aspects range from the type of employees it recruits to the company's profit margins. This categorizing approach makes sense, as the era of globalization facilitates the side by side existence of manufacturers, product- and solutions-based companies. The objective in this book was to explain the advantages and limitations of each type of company type, and to offer a new formula for distinguishing between the various types. If, until now, the way of distinguishing company types used terms such as marketing vs. production-bound companies, the current manuscript suggests that it is time to alter the terms of the discussion. In the current day and age, production-bound companies will soon find themselves in the manufacturer's rubric, while marketing-bound companies are finding it necessary to close down their production departments and out-source this service. The world is demanding more and more solutions: the more complex the world becomes, the more clients are willing to pay for a complete solution, without having to work at building its components. Hence, more and more companies will seek to operate as solutions-based companies.

A few hundred years ago, each person had the means to produce food for subsistence: fields of grain and live-stock for eggs, milk and meat. The world has moved on since then, and people began buying these from the shop. The revolution of processed food provided a solution for a world defined by time constraints: instead of spending time on preparing food from scratch, it is now possible to purchase almost any food either readymade or pre-processed. The process took a lot of time to evolve, but currently industrial food is in greater demand than are primary ingredients. The next phase of the revolution was the dissemination of the culture of buying ready-made meals. Currently there are many families who hardly prepare food at home, but purchase all their meals –including the serving utensils – from the nearest food vendor. The current stage of the food revolution focuses on healthy food. The world has come to understand that the transition to fast food was done at the expense of nutritional values; consequently, today the trend is make this readymade food healthy. The next stage will be for companies to adopt the subscriber model, whereby fresh food will be pre-ordered from a fixed menu or according to the client's preferences and delivered at predetermined times. In addition, companies will also stock the client's refrigerator with fresh produce and foods, according to the customer's tastes and preferences.

The ubiquity of solutions-based companies in the food and nutrition industry will symbolize the last stage before seeking full automation. The wish to pass on the responsibility for the house chores to others, for a fee already is the norm in many of the bountiful societies in the world. The task of feeding household members will be the next overall solution to be supplied by specialized companies. After reading the chapter on pricing, it will come as no surprise that the price of food provided by a feeding solutions company that has a network of subscribers can be cheaper than the amount a regular family spends on food. The percentage of ingredients wasted on passed due dates will be smaller, and the ability to pre-order a fixed amount of food rather than gambling on consumption trends with each purchase will save both food and expenses.

As the example of the food industry demonstrates, there is no industry in the world that will not need to move towards a solutions-based paradigm. The evolution from a subsistence-based to an industrial economy and from there on to knowledge-intensive industries suggests that the next step in the industrial revolution will be from a product-based to a solutions-based industry. This shift does not depend on any single individual or organized group of persons, but on human beings as a collective: we just want to make our lives easier.

Epilogue

After I returned from my vacation in Thailand, I met again with Ner's managers and used the manufacturing – product-based – solutions-based model to explain my decision. It became clear that I would not work in Ner in its current status, since my relative strength could not be properly utilized in a manufacturing company. However, since the owners still wanted to cooperate with me, they offered me to participate in a new project, which would combine Ner's manufacturing abilities and my abilities in business development and marketing.

After some back-and-forth and discussions, we established the joint project. Ner invested the establishment and operational costs, and had the major share of the project. The aim was to develop new markets and products, using Ner's specific abilities. The project was operated from Ner's premises, in order to reduce costs and use the existing extensive infrastructure. My concern was what would happen as soon as there would be conflict between the new project's objectives and those of Ner. What if the project developed a product and another company asked Ner to produce it? This should be a conflict of interest for Ner. Ostensibly, as part-owners of a product-based endeavor, Ner's owners should prefer to find a manufacturer that would do the job for a lower price. It wouldn't make sense to try and have it both ways, but would Ner turn down the job?

The first test came soon enough. The first product I worked on was an adaptation of a product that Ner had manufactured for a regular repeat customer, in other words, a customer that brought in a significant share of Ner's annual sales. After I had worked on developing the product, experimented with potential clients and had run R&D tests, on one occasion, the same customer was on Ner's premises and saw a brochure for the new adapted product which was competing with its own product. The client immediately informed them that unless Ner stopped developing the new product, it would no longer bring its manufacturing business to Ner. The threat worked, and Ner decided that "a bird in the hand was worth two in the bush" and discontinued that product.

I decided to develop another product, for which Ner had the some manufacturing experience, although not at the level of the final product. After investing time and knowledge in this product, I brought Ner the knowledge and required equipment to make the whole product. This advanced Ner's manufacturing capabilities and enabled it to supply its clients with better quality products. Ner's sales people were encouraged by the ability to produce at a higher level, and began marketing this enhanced ability, developed by the project. In fact, they offered the same products as the project, but at Ner's pricing schedule. This effectively undermined the project: Ner was offering the same knowledge at lower prices, and the project simply couldn't compete with Ner's pricing and remain afloat. Obviously, the first big order went to Ner.

Shortly after, I met with Ner's CEO, who made it clear that although the ability to manufacture the product was the result of my efforts, and the knowledge in fact belonged to the project, the project was not entitled to any share of the profits from this first order, since the order went to Ner, and the profit margins were not high enough to share with the project.

As soon as I understood that Ner would continue to operate as a manufacturing company, while the project would develop products and pass the knowledge on to Ner, it became clear that the project could never be profitable. In order to end the project, I met with the owners and announced that although, by contract, the project may continue, it was not fiscally justifiable as long as it was Ner's second priority. The project was stopped after only five months of activity with no profit, but I had gained many insights from the experience.

The first insight was that the theory presented in this book was correct. I had always applied these categories, but having firsthand experience of the tense interactions between the manufacturing and the product-based company gave me a chance to see precisely how it works.

The second insight was that one must listen to the instincts and gut-feelings. My instinct was not to enter Ner in any form, but after meeting the owners, who are very nice people, I was blinded by their kind approach and decided to accept the offer and go into partnership with them. In hindsight it is clear that there was no place for such a partnership. The owners are wonderful people, accustomed to the world of manufacturing. Thus, for a manufacturing company, even when embarking on a new initiative, the new venture is expected to be profitable from day one. Turning down an opportunity for profit due to strategic considerations is not part of the culture of a manufacturing company.

My third insight was that in order to use my skills to the best of my ability, I would need to be involved in creating innovative products and produce solutions.

After finishing this joint project, I dedicated myself to working in the firm I have owned since 2007, where I develop innovative products and solutions. In the course of my work I found a wonderful partner-investor, who left me free to create patents and solutions. My advantage is my creative thinking, which is expressed in the invention of things that make our lives better, or in thinking up business theories.

I hope you enjoyed reading the book as much as I enjoyed writing it.

Sincerely,

Netanel Raisch

PS – I will be happy to hear your feedback and insights and I will try to answer any question regarding the book at www.netanelraisch.com

www.ingramcontent.com/pod-product-compliance
Lightning Source LLC
Chambersburg PA
CBHW071411170526
45165CB00001B/242